NCE F

Leapfrog

"*Leapfrog*'s scrappy yet sophisticated advice helps aspiring entrepreneurs from all backgrounds understand how to be the CEOs of our own lives and the creators of our destinies."

—JAMIA WILSON, executive director and publisher,
Feminist Press, City University of New York

"A must-have for every woman, budding entrepreneur or not. [It's] packed with practical and relevant advice—you can't help but be emboldened to take that first step toward making your business idea a reality."

—JACKI ZEHNER, chief engagement officer and cofounder of
Women Moving Millions

"For those of us who don't have an MBA or a million-dollar network to pave the way, we have Nathalie's helpful hacks to catapult us into the C-suite and beyond."

—RUTHIE ACKERMAN, deputy editor of Women@Forbes

"There is hidden money and opportunity in America. Nathalie provides the shortcuts to solve the puzzle and go get it!"

—NELY GALÁN, author of *New York Times*–bestselling *Self Made:
Becoming Empowered, Self-Reliant, and Rich in Every Way*

"Filled with practical advice for real women on everything from funding to finding a network; Nathalie understands that women want to build from the heart, and that how you get there is just as important as where you're going."

—DANIELLE KAYEMBE, author of
The Silent Rise of the Female-Driven Economy

"I believe everyone has the entrepreneurial spirit within them—the information and inspiration within *Leapfrog* will serve to empower all women for generations to come."

—NINA VACA, founder, chairman, and CEO, Pinnacle Group

"With Nathalie Molina Niño's help, maybe we can finally thwart the system that has kept women from thriving."

—MARIE C. WILSON, honorary founder and president emerita,
Ms. Foundation for Women; founder and president emerita,
The White House Project; advisory board chair, VoteRunLead

"The new playbook for the modern entrepreneur who is redefining success on her own terms. Nathalie is clearly rooting for all of us."

—TIFFANY DUFU, tiffanydufu.com

"Bring your best game—the road map is in your hands."

—LOLA C. WEST, managing director, WestFuller Advisors LLC

"A definite must-read for any woman entrepreneur serious about scaling."

—MELANIE HAWKEN, Lionesses of Africa

"In her brilliant new book, Nathalie Molina Niño shares the indispensable advice that's helped her guide women entrepreneurs from zero to scalable and thriving businesses—and can transform yours as well."

—Dorie Clark, adjunct professor,
Duke University Fuqua School of Business

"*Leapfrog* cuts through the typical 'lift yourself up by your bootstraps' advice . . . to get to the delicious truth of the hustle that is possible for entrepreneurs often locked out of the system."

—KAT COLE, COO and president, North America, Focus Brands

"If you have this book, it will change your life, whether you are on an entrepreneurial path or just dreaming of taking the leap."

—WHITNEY SMITH, chief of strategy
and brand at The Dream Corps

"I cannot recommend *Leapfrog* too highly—it's the secret weapon we all need in the face of rich white male privilege to help level the entrepreneurial playing field."

—CINDY GALLOP, founder and CEO, MakeLoveNotPorn

"Nathalie Molina Niño has finally given us the book we've been wanting about women entrepreneurs in the twenty-first century."

—JIMMIE BRIGGS, cofounder, Man Up Campaign,
NYC Gender Equity Commission

LEAPFROG

The New Revolution for Women Entrepreneurs

NATHALIE MOLINA NIÑO

with Sara Grace

A TarcherPerigee Book

An imprint of Penguin Random House LLC
375 Hudson Street
New York, New York 10014

TarcherPerigee with tp colophon is a registered trademark of Penguin Random House LLC.

Most TarcherPerigee books are available at special quantity discounts for bulk purchase for sales promotions, premiums, fund-raising, and educational needs. Special books or book excerpts also can be created to fit specific needs. For details, write: SpecialMarkets@penguinrandomhouse.com.

Library of Congress Cataloging-in-Publication Data

Names: Molina Niño, Nathalie, author. | Grace, Sara, author.
Title: Leapfrog : the new revolution for women entrepreneurs / Nathalie Molina Niño, Sara Grace.
Description: First Edition. | New York : TarcherPerigee, 2018. | Includes bibliographical references. |
Identifiers: LCCN 2018009313 (print) | LCCN 2018012981 (ebook) | ISBN 9780525503927 (e-book) | ISBN 9780143132202 (paperback)
Subjects: LCSH: Businesswomen. | Entrepreneurship. | BISAC: BUSINESS & ECONOMICS / Entrepreneurship. | BUSINESS & ECONOMICS / Motivational.
Classification: LCC HD6053 (ebook) | LCC HD6053 .M586 2018 (print) | DDC 658.4/21082—dc23
LC record available at https://lccn.loc.gov/2018009313

Printed in the United States of America
1 3 5 7 9 10 8 6 4 2

Book design by Katy Riegel

Contents

SECTION 2 HACKS: SET

SECTION 3 HACKS: GO

SECTION 4 HACKS: FUND

SECTION 5 HACKS: GROW

Foreword

NATHALIE MOLINA NIÑO is a fierce friend and tireless advocate known for getting things done. The organization I founded and lead, Black Girls CODE, has benefitted many times from Nathalie's indefatigable willingness to connect, advocate, and shout until the impossible is done. Today, any Lyft rider can instantly donate to Black Girls CODE thanks, in part, to Nathalie's stepping up and making a connection—just one of the many items added to her completed to-do list. I've been happy to support her, as well, during critical leaps, like when I flew to the White House to help her announce her newly launched company at South by South Lawn in 2016. And I was equally happy to join her here, now, in the pages of this book.

One of my favorite moments with Nathalie, one that I found myself remembering as I read *Leapfrog*, was backstage at New York Fashion Week in 2015 to participate in Carrie Hammer's Role Models Not Runway Models™ show. Hair and makeup were done and the audience started to pile into the space. We were moments from starting and I looked around and noticed no one was the color they were born. Many, many of us had turned anxious shades of strange hues. The pre-show panic and jitters were in full effect and I found myself, like everyone else, incredibly nervous. Everyone, that is, but Nathalie, who was brimming with excitement and offered up a pep talk that shifted everything.

She reminded me I wasn't there for me. I was there for the girls I have the honor to serve.

She said it didn't matter if the hair and makeup were any good, or if I walked down the runway looking like a pro or a hot mess. What mattered is that I was there for the girls, the ones who rarely see anyone who looks like them on any runway, in any fashion week. Now, don't for a second think Nathalie was not prepared for a moment such as this. After her spirited pep talk and a few makeup touch-ups for us both, we strutted down that runway like nobody's business.

That same bounce in your step, readers, is what you're going to walk away with after reading this book. Nathalie has made it her life's work to be a relentless champion for people she believes in. The stories and brass-tack hacks in this book are no different from that backstage pep talk, only these were assembled for you. *You* are the ones she believes in.

But your own success is only the beginning. Nathalie reminds us in every hack that it's in our capable hands to clear the path for the women and girls who will come next. We owe it to them to be impatient and demand not one but several seats at the table, and I for one can't wait to see what *you* do, now that it's your turn to leapfrog into your big, bad entrepreneurial dreams.

—Kimberly Bryant

Introduction

Patience Is *Not* a Virtue

LEAPFROG: (v.) To work around, leap over, or outsmart anything that gets in the way of succeeding as an entrepreneur, on your terms. (n.) Any hack used to leapfrog; a clever, ethical means of leveling the playing field.

When I was growing up, I watched my Ecuadorian grandmother, my *abuelita* Blanca, work herself to the bone every day until late at night. She was a strong, bold woman whose best opportunity was amid the loud din of the sweatshops of Los Angeles.

One night when I was about eight, I decided to ask the *abuelita* I so adored to teach *me* to sew. I was my grandmother's favorite; she would do anything I threw at her. Yet when I made this request, it felt as though I'd made the proverbial record player come to a screeching halt. She stopped her work, shut off the machine, and turned her entire body to face me. I didn't know what I had done, but I was terrified.

"No, *mija*," she said slowly, with fire in her eyes. "I work so that you will never have to earn a living with your hands."

I'll be damned, she was telling me, *if you waste a scrap of the opportunity I'm creating by thinking small or looking backward.* The work she did was honorable; there is no shame in making a living with your hands. But it was my job in life to work as smart as she did hard, so that I could achieve goals far beyond the reach of anyone attached to a machine twelve hours a day.

I didn't have a word for it then, or any understanding, but I do now. My grandmother was telling me to look forward and up—to *leapfrog* my family to new heights. This was her immigrant dream.

Several decades and a lot of my own battle scars later, I want to help others leapfrog. I've seen the need. Maybe you've tried reading advice about bootstrapping a business and thought, "Um . . . so where are my bootstraps?" Or maybe you've heard stories about startups receiving millions in funding—but noticed that most of the founders are either men or Ivy League grads and wondered whether everyone else was shut out. This book is for you.

Women receive just 2.5 percent of venture capital (VC) funding—and of those, about 0.2 percent are women of color. Women simply don't have access to the capital that men do. Bärí A. Williams, from online ticket supplier StubHub, once summed it up this way: "White men get funded on ideas. White women get funded on results. Black women receive no funding."[1]

I recently spoke on a panel of women investors to a packed room of both women and men eager to talk about how to get to gender parity in business. As we talked about market trends we'd been seeing, I mentioned one that seems at odds with the stats just mentioned: Black women and Latinx are starting companies at a faster rate than anyone else in this country. In fact, 78 percent of new women-owned firms are started by women of color.[2] When we got to the Q&A period, a wise woman in the front row directed a question to one of my co-panelists, a woman who runs a fund that invests in early-stage, women-led businesses, largely in tech.

"You said today that you've invested in more than sixty companies," she said. "Nathalie was talking about how women of color are starting companies more than anyone else in this country.

How many of your sixty-plus companies are led by women of color?"

If you identify with what I've written so far, I doubt you'll be surprised to hear the answer: *Big. Fat. Zero.*

Big fat zero is a big fat problem. Women—and women of color in particular—are starting businesses like crazy, but they rarely grow beyond supporting their owner, too small to court investment. In the case of my co-panelist who funds women-owned startups, the problem is more complex than simply turning down women of color. She has a pipeline problem that goes beyond race. The entrepreneurs making it into VC conference rooms represent a tiny, privileged sliver of women. They are mostly white and well-off, with institutions like HBS, Goldman, or Google on their résumés.

They're still kickass founders, and funds like my co-panelist's are doing important work. But if you're like most women, you have no idea how you're going to get into *any* investor's office. You probably haven't grown beyond solopreneurship or the side hustle because you've got one or all of these problems:

- You don't have personal capital—tens of thousands of dollars in a rainy-day fund—or the spare time to spot opportunities, strategize, and think big.
- You don't have friends or family who can invest their money or contribute key resources, like time with the family lawyer or a rent-free place to live.
- You didn't go to fancy schools, so you don't have ready-made networks and cultural capital to create the client and marketing relationships that would help you jump to the next level.

Without these assets, many bright, entrepreneurial women get stuck in what I have started to call the Valley of Death—that long stretch between a one-woman show and a scalable business that becomes a household name. Many women never make the shift to entrepreneur at all. We're too busy paying rent or putting food on the table.

This opportunity gap is why I founded BRAVA Investments. We invest in companies not based on whether they have women founders but on whether they can prove that they will economically benefit as many women as possible. My goal isn't to find a woman and make her into the next Zuckerbergian billionaire so much as it's to find companies that can level the playing field for a *billion* women. I want companies that can change systems, by putting money and power in the pockets of many women so they can be armed with those bootstraps everyone's so fond of romanticizing. Only then will we see women begin to rival men in building companies that change the future of their families and the world.

But I'm impatient, one of my better qualities. So one day I started thinking: BRAVA is important because it attacks the systemic problem, but how do I help the women who are ready to be entrepreneurs *today*? How do I help all of *them* make it past the Valley of Death?

I started thinking about something I had seen in South America. In the Andes, where my family is from, indigenous farmers who never had a landline now walk around with two smartphones in their pockets, a technological advance that has allowed them to bank, shop, and even sell their products and services to anyone in the world. They have *leapfrogged* what outsiders would have thought were absolute limitations on their potential.

And so I started to ask myself—and soon, every entrepreneur I knew—a question: What would be the equivalent of two smartphones in the pockets of every woman in this country who wanted to beat the odds to build and grow a business?

From there *Leapfrog* was born, a compilation of the best hacks I've come across to work around, leap over, or straight-up annihilate the seemingly intractable hurdles facing those of you trying to cross the Valley of Death, or bootstrap without bootstraps. Funny thing, when I called on my community to help me home in on a title, lots of women had negative reactions to the very idea of leapfrogging. Whether I explained them as *shortcuts* or *hacks*, more than a few of my friends started nail-biting about whether I was encouraging people to skip steps or to use some sort of trick to jump from the back of the line to the front.

These people are conscientious. They want to play fair, or they are so used to bumping into the rules other people have prescribed for them, as women and/or people of color, that they are on a short tether. I get it. But this attitude is part of the problem.

Here are the facts: Successful people take shortcuts all the damn time. They're called trust funds. Or nepotism, the likes of which are boldly on display in the Oval Office of the forty-fifth U.S. president. Or legacies, if you're talking about kids who get into the Ivy League because of their last names, not their SAT scores.

Instead of pretending those shortcuts don't exist and that many successful people don't benefit from them daily, I'd rather be in the business of making sure more of us know and understand how they work. Leapfrog, shortcut, hack—let's just call it what women need to do in order to get their fair shot, and get it now.

It's time to shift your thinking. What follows is the ethos that informs what I think of as a leapfrogger's mind-set.

1. **We aren't ashamed to hack.** Hacks aren't so much about cutting in line as identifying gaps to fill and taking our shots, rather than waiting for them to be offered. Women believe they have to play by the rules, as Tara Mohr, the author of *Playing Big*, discovered while surveying women about what holds them back. Playing by the rules and waiting to be rewarded for doing so is how we get stuck playing small—in lower-paying jobs and in a headspace where we lack the audacity to leapfrog into entrepreneurship.

2. **This country was built on the backs of women and people of color.** We deserve a spot in that line with everyone else.

Wait to be bumped from the back, and you'll be waiting forever.

3. **We favor outcomes over optics.** Getting a few more Marissa Mayers to the helms of big companies like Yahoo! won't magically resolve the gender-wage gap any more than getting a black man in the Oval Office solved racism in America. These often become little more than symbols. It's important to put more women in the C-suite, but it's unfair to think that that will solve the persistent problems most women face. We can't pay the rent with symbols. We can't feed our children with tokens. Cash is king. So let's move the conversation away from tokenism and symbols and down to real results we can all take to the bank.

4. **Impatience is a virtue.** I don't want to be on another panel in ten years, have an audience member ask, "How many women of color?," and have the answer be two instead of zero. But if we keep doing what we've always done, "progress" will putter along as it has for decades, pointing to a future in which U.S. women don't achieve pay parity with men for another *134 years*.[3] The next generation needs us to be impatient. Impatient with every injustice that still remains and with every BS story that is still being told about what we can and can't do. They're relying on us, and I'm not about to let anyone tell me that a shortcut is a bad thing. Our time is well overdue, and if anyone has a problem with the fact that we want to find faster, cheaper, better ways to get there, they can just take a seat and watch us. And if it gets us called *bitchy*, *difficult*, and *unruly*, let's see these for what they are: magnetic success traits that have propelled plenty of men to the top. Because we can't wait to be given equality; we have to take what's ours. And we have every right to be impatient about it.

THE TROUBLE WITH 99 PERCENT OF BUSINESS ADVICE

Much of the typical advice and success stories in glossy magazines and business how-tos don't work for everyone. Of course, they're not positioned as being for only a privileged few, but in many instances, good luck trying to apply the lessons if you're not white, rich, and male. Here are five examples:

1. **"Don't go to college."** Wealthy, expensively educated white men like Peter Thiel and James Altucher (Stanford and Cornell, respectively) have recommended that young entrepreneurs skip college or drop out—arguably OK advice if your social or economic background provides ample influence and cultural capital. It's a tougher sell for someone coming in as an outsider, without the bona fides of privilege. While the traditional four-year university isn't for everyone, education (in its various forms) has historically been the most prevalent, successful leapfrog. I may have dropped out of college at twenty-one, but attending an elite Los Angeles prep school—a huge sacrifice for my family—and later a prestigious Ivy League school gave me cultural capital that I'm still spending every day.

2. **"Change the world with social entrepreneurship."** I love a business that makes money while solving a specific social problem—but don't let the search for this kind of synergy distract you from moving forward on a great idea. Your first focus needs to be finding a business idea that solves an acute customer problem and meets a clear demand. And PS, *every* business is social entrepreneurship if you can bring living wages to a community where few have access to them.

3. **"Turn your passion into a business."** As my friend Nely Galán writes in her book *Self Made*, "Follow your bliss is BS!" Make something that people want, and then use your fat bank account to indulge your passion.

4. **"As CEO, pay yourself last."** Say what?! How am I supposed to run a business and still feed myself without an income, a trust fund, or any kind of safety net?
5. **"Support yourself with part-time work while you launch."** Great advice—unless you're barely making ends meet working sixty-plus hours a week.

It goes on and on. The challenge of building a company without capital is real, and I'm going to be honest with you: No book can fully solve it. (Hence, BRAVA.) But here I've called upon everyone I know who has gone from zero to scalable business to share their best secrets; you'll learn about their personal experiences with loopholes and shortcuts that work even if you aren't starting with money, cultural capital, or connections. The people you'll read about aren't all women, and they aren't all leapfroggers. In life as in business, we'll get a lot further, faster if we don't limit ourselves to a fraction of the talent pool. We're here to share, borrow, and steal all the best hacks to move ourselves forward.

WHY ME? THE ONLY LATINX IN THE ROOM

I was raised with love by immigrant entrepreneurs and got my MBA at the family dinner table. My grandmother, who I introduced earlier, worked hard enough to eventually help her children own their own apparel and textile factories. I've spent most of my career in tech. I dropped out of college after the scrappy web development company I founded with two partners in Boulder, Colorado, ballooned into a real business. It was in the very early days of the commercial internet, and we made large-scale, database-driven, transactional websites for companies. We were all self-taught, and there was no sense that it wasn't a woman's space. I had no frame of reference, it was fun, and it let me exercise my love of design. (I had studied engineering but was an artist at heart.)

I eventually started six more ventures, of which BRAVA is the sixth. When I exited venture number two, I grew and ran a multinational business across sixteen countries before turning twenty-five. In my last tech adventure, I used crowdsourcing to help companies like Google and Bing improve their algorithms in more than sixty languages. After fifteen years working with every tech and media giant in the world, from Seattle to Mumbai, Tokyo, Dublin and back, I didn't just get tired of being the only woman in the room; I got tired of being the only Latinx in the building.

I reached a point in my career where I wanted to pay it forward. While I had been successful in tech, I felt that I hadn't done enough to leave it a better place for women than I found it. So I cofounded a center for women entrepreneurs at Barnard College's Athena Center for Leadership Studies and spent more than five years teaching, advocating for women in tech, and advising early-stage, women-led startups. Over time, it became clear to me that no amount of mentoring and education could resolve the largest issue holding women back: lack of capital. So I founded BRAVA.

And yet when it comes to writing this book, I've got something much more important than my own experiences: I've got what investors call *deal-flow*, which means I'm good at finding and building relationships with creative, interesting, groundbreaking entrepreneurs. In my work at BRAVA—and before that, years of supporting women in tech—I spend every day hunting them down, with a particular interest in leapfroggers. Every day I meet someone who's done something incredible, something that no one would have expected he or she could ever accomplish. People like:

- Arlan Hamilton, who was sleeping on the floor of San Francisco's airport when she finally signed the first investor to Backstage Capital, her fund focused on women-, people of color-, and LGBT-led businesses.

- John Henry, a black Latinx doorman who started a dry-cleaning delivery service, grew it to fifteen employees, built an app, and then was acquired for $1 million by one of his vendors—all by the age of twenty-one.
- Kat Cole, who started her career as a Hooters waitress and became the president of Cinnabon and now the COO of Focus Brands, the parent company to Cinnabon, Auntie Anne's, and Carvel, among others, which together have supported thousands of new entrepreneurs by offering affordable franchise business opportunities.

Your story can and should one day be worthy of such a list. Use this book to support you as you leap higher and faster than anyone—including we ourselves—thinks possible. Find the opportunities and alternate paths that others miss. And when you find a hack that's *not* in this book, head to leapfroghacks.com and pay it forward with your story.

We don't need one female Mark Zuckerberg, or even a dozen. We need an army of *you*s, and I am honored to give you fifty leapfrogs to help you get there faster.

Ready

Entrepreneurship is a marathon. Every "overnight success story" you read about was inevitably preceded by a decade or more of hustling, too long and complex a story for your average news article. There's work that has to happen long before you lace up your shoes on race day—practical skills development, logistics, but also mental training. You have to be able to imagine yourself both running and finishing the race. You also need to build the stamina to fuel years of hustle.

This pregame is critical for women, and even more so for women of color. Women function within a system that was not built for us. The business world was made for dads with wives who raised the kids and frosted the cakes. By design, we're square pegs in round holes. Long term, we have to change the systems. But right now, tomorrow, when you wake up in the morning, the reality is that you have to hack the system as it is. You have to make up the shortfall between what you've been handed in this world and what you're demanding of it. No one else will.

Hack 1

You Don't Need a Hoodie

When I think about the entrepreneurs I most admire, they aren't code-jockey bros hunched over keyboards in hoodies. They aren't neurotic geniuses obsessed with Mars or how to extend their life with robotic parts. They're not hyperfocused on how they'll "exit" as fast as possible with a big wad of cash. They're also not trust-fund kids who don't really care whether they're actually making an impact or even supporting themselves.

The entrepreneurs I most admire are those who many would never pick out of a lineup as a hotshot. Ignoring everyone else's expectations, plugging away without promise of glory or quick reward, they committed to playing big—and won. There are more of them than you think. Some are driven by an Oprah-esque impulse to dominate an industry or become a global icon. Others want to solve problems, small or large. Still others want to give their children more opportunities than their grandparents ever imagined. What they all have in common is a desire to build something greater than a livelihood for themselves. And so they poured their energies into creating businesses that in turn created jobs, spread ideas they held dear, lifted up their communities, and, yes, allowed them to stop having to worry about whether they could pay rent.

So if you want to start a business but look nothing like the "entrepreneur" you're picturing, stop worrying. You're in good company. But it's up to you to rewrite what you may have thought were the rules. You're not going to succeed unless you believe that your way of doing things is as right as anybody else's.

Have you ever:

- Solved a problem that made someone's day a little easier?
- Inspired someone to help you or help themselves?
- Made someone laugh with a funny story?
- Made do with less of something than you needed?
- Organized an event, from a kid's birthday party to a fundraiser?
- Had an epic failure and bounced back?

If the answer to most of those was yes, congratulations! You have everything you need to succeed as an entrepreneur.

Nothing in that list seems gendered, right? And yet so many women hear *entrepreneur* and immediately think *not me*. Well, no wonder. The headlines of late have been dominated by what you might call *flippers*: (mostly) young men creating digital assets that attract funding from rich venture capitalists, then sell for millions of dollars while their work is reduced to some lines of code to live inside someone else's software, padding the bank accounts of a handful of people who are already rich.

Business media toss around words like *genius, disruption,* and *exit strategy* and celebrate people who may be visionary but are also almost uniformly men. So of course entrepreneurship becomes "other." Of course we feel like imposters. Of course we lose our confidence.

But what if entrepreneurship isn't any of those things? What if it could be *service? Collaboration? Community?* Real entrepreneurs are caretakers as much as they are visionaries—and they can do it while "making an absolute shit ton of money," as advertising legend Cindy Gallop likes to say. "The future is doing good and making money simultaneously."

What if I also told you women own 36 percent of all businesses in the United States? That includes only 13 percent of middle-market firms—companies with revenue between $10 million and $1 billion—but that's changing, fast. Women-owned companies are entering the middle market at eight times the rate of businesses in general.[1]

You have every right to make a new story around the word *entrepreneur*. Rewrite it to fit your lifestyle and values. I am a fan of the Core 10, a manifesto of leadership principles we developed at Barnard's Athena Center for Leadership Studies. As you build your business, hold the Core 10—the first, the foundational hack—close.

THE CORE 10

Adapted from Barnard's Athena Center for Leadership Studies' Core 10

1. **Vision.** Hell yeah, you're a visionary. You envision a bigger piece of the pie for you, your family, and your community. Good for you.
2. **Ambition.** Too many people, particularly women, think *ambitious* is another way of saying *ruthless*. Ambition is the desire to do what it takes to create impact, the *responsibility* to be strategic and stretch every minute and dollar with as many shortcuts as you can find.
3. **Courage.** Be bold, and take risks. Maybe you've heard that women are more risk-averse than men. Bullshit. Studies show women are willing to take big risks when the payoff is big impact.[2]

4. **Entrepreneurial Spirit.** Imaginative, flexible, and persistent—these qualities define my mother and all the other mothers I know. You don't survive kids without them! But this is a special gift of women in general. We've always found ways to make lemonade from lemons. Stay scrappy.

5. **Resilience.** Get comfortable with things being hard, really hard. That's the reality of starting a business. Likewise, get comfortable with screwing up. Don't just survive failure. Love it, own it, learn from it.

6. **Communication.** Business advice—historically written by men, for men—has typically overemphasized active communication: the words you say, how you say them, when you say them. But communication also requires silence: yours. You need to listen just as actively as you speak—and not just listen but invite honesty, beg for it when you need to, and be open to what you hear.

7. **Leverage.** Sitting at tables of white men in suits, I hear the word *leverage* all the time. It's part of a power game, moving forward an agenda by sheer force. Not anymore. Leverage is recognizing that you alone can't get a damn thing done. Leverage is your ability to send an email and get a helpful response in ten minutes. Leverage is mobilizing your squad (which of course can include men).

8. **Collaboration.** Women are known for being astute collaborators. Collaboration, not command-and-control, is considered the gold standard in getting things done in today's complex, interdependent world. Good news, ladies: We're finally trending.

9. **Negotiation.** Negotiation isn't two hungry dogs who want the same bone. It's two parties putting their heads together to find a bigger snack. Approach the negotiating table with the attitude that your objective is to bridge a difference,

not fight for your turf. You'll be immediately more confident that you're the most qualified negotiator at the table.

10. **Advocacy.** Set your sights on being a builder, not a flipper. As you grow your business and rise as a leader, pay it forward. Raise your mic and extend your hand, always, for those who don't yet have a voice.

Hack 2

Don't Mourn; Organize

IT's NOT EASY starting a business as a woman, especially if you are also a person of color. You are likely to be underestimated. You're probably carrying more of the responsibility at home—maybe all the responsibility. You might be starting with even fewer resources and less access than your peers.

Well, screw all that. To borrow a phrase from the labor movement: Don't mourn; organize. Move beyond the paralysis of sadness to the productivity of anger. Let righteousness become the fuel you need to ignore the standard rules, statistics, and expectations, and hack *your* way to success, whatever that looks like.

When I was in my early twenties in college in Boulder, Colorado, having that attitude set my life on an entirely new course. The story I always tell people is that I dropped out of school because my web development business took off and I struggled to balance that with homework. The truth is more complicated.

As a student in Boulder, I started a web development company by accident. The idea came after I wiped out on my motorcycle and needed to buy a car. I started my search on the then-nascent internet. Very quickly I found out that few of the dealerships in town had a website. It didn't take a genius to see an opportunity.

I walked down the east end of Pearl Street where all the car lots were, picked the most mom-and-pop-looking one, and pitched its owner. Would he sell me a car half price if I built his business a website? I drove away that day in an old Jeep Cherokee, beat up but functional, and a lot safer than my old ride.

Soon I was building sites for his friends, other small-time car dealers. The company grew quickly, so I brought on two friends as partners. We graduated to building sites that were much more than advertisements. They were the backbone of entirely new businesses, with complex back-end databases and user platforms.

At the time, we *were* Boulder's tech scene. We had an office and hired employees as we took on new projects. We were crazy busy, and it became clear we needed to add more staff. Meanwhile, I was still juggling the business with the life I had so carefully planned: finishing college and getting a PhD in environmental engineering. (My immigrant parents had made clear that there were only three appropriate careers for their child: doctor, lawyer, or engineer.) I had set my sights on a university in New Zealand.

It was a stressful time, but my inner control freak was thriving. I was bringing a new level of professionalism to our business as we grew. I shifted from coding to being the person who wrote the proposals, negotiated the deals, and communicated with customers. (Neither of my coder partners was interested in these tasks.) It was exciting and demanding, and I was loving it.

And then the universe stepped up, cleared her throat, and said, "*No*, Nathalie."

It started in the form of a hunch that led me to schedule a gynecology appointment months before I was due for my annual pap. The nice Chilean doctor listened to my concern and, despite the fact that everything had been normal just months before, agreed to test me. Two weeks later, when the results came in, I was diagnosed with cervical cancer. Within another week, my mom was flying in to be with me during surgery to remove a big chunk of my cervix.

Recovery was more onerous and stressful than the surgery. There were lots of questions about the follow-up treatment. Radiation? Chemo? The doctors couldn't give me any statistics; at only twenty years old, I was an anomaly outside their data set. I started considering alternative holistic paths, since no one really seemed sure what was best.

Well, one person seemed sure: my mother, who pressured me to move home to Los Angeles, where she and my dad's network (doctors, friends, even naturopaths!) could take care of me. At this point, my schoolwork started to suffer, and it became clear that I had three choices. I could put a hold on everything, accept I was sick, and return to the warm womb of my family in Los Angeles— never happening. I could give up the business. Or I could recalibrate what I thought my life was going to look like. Bye, bye, New Zealand and the clear, orderly path to success as I had defined it. I didn't know exactly what the business would become—what the internet would become—but I had a hunch and was learning to follow my instincts. I also knew that I had created something out of nothing and seemed to be pretty good at it.

When the universe knocks you over, you can become undone, retreating to lick your wounds and rebuild your story along familiar lines. Or you can choose to get organized. Evaluate your priorities, be pragmatic, make choices, and break ground on a new, more promising path that may look nothing like what you had envisioned for yourself.

So I withdrew from school, expecting to feel grief as I let that dream go. None came. I had recognized my limitations, taken stock, and committed to a focused course of action. The business became more important than ever because I had given up something significant for it. I felt the giddy exhilaration of the power that comes when you make choices that are truly your own— whatever limits others may try to impose.

And when the life cycle of that business and those partnerships ran its course, once again, I didn't mourn. I organized. By that time, no one wanted to buy a web development business. Competition was popping up everywhere, and we had little to differentiate ourselves. We did have something, though: intellectual property. Every contract our clients signed clearly stated that we owned the code. While a web development company wasn't valuable, the code we had contributed to a number of our clients' businesses was. And so I sold the technology in parts. It pissed off at least one of my former clients, but he had signed the contract, so it really didn't matter how anybody felt about it.

It all added up to my first entrepreneurial win, a pretty good one for a twenty-three-year-old college dropout. I took my experience and used it to move to Seattle and build a business with a subsidiary of one of the oldest publicly traded companies in the U.S., Bowne Global Solutions (BGS). We were globalizing digital content, like Encarta, which we translated into ten different languages. I was off and running, using my experience as an entrepreneur to test the waters as an intrapreneur.

Leapfroggers don't fall prey to the paralysis of bitterness or sorrow. When they get shafted, they turn anger into energy. When things go sideways, that energy becomes the fuel for their creativity and drive. In the words of *Ebony* founder John H. Johnson, "When I see a barrier, I cry and I curse, and then I get a ladder and climb over it."

Is the universe (or the people in it) giving you resistance? Go out and use that energy to demand you get your shot. Ask for unpublished opportunities and special consideration. Be crafty and adaptable. Make necessity the mother of your reinvention. You'll get plenty of *no*s—but they become more oxygen for the flame of action.

Don't mourn; organize.

Hack 3

Take Daily Vacations

EVERYONE FEELS SHORT on money, time, and imagination at times. The traditional solution is to look forward to a vacation once or twice a year. But you, you're launching a business, and so you have a problem: *Every single day* you're short on money, time, and, if you're not careful, imagination.

The cognitive load of launching a business is huge. You're making decisions under pressure and amid scarcity. Financial worries can cripple decision-making even more than other kinds of worries, according to recent studies on what you might call poverty PTSD. Maybe you've also read the research showing that court judges make different decisions on sentencing depending on whether they've had their lunch yet. (Scary.) Our bodies need careful tending if they're to produce strong and consistent decisions.

On top of all this, an entrepreneur needs *more* imagination every day than other folks. It's how you solve the weird problems that are particular to the absurd and wonderful project of trying to build something from nothing.

So forget the annual vacation model. It no longer fits your life, and you probably don't have paid vacation time anyway. Instead, hack a vacation into *every single day*. Every single day you need to carve out some space for self-reflection and peace. Here are a few ideas on how to make this happen.

- **Commit.** Having a grounding force in your life is the secret to being relentlessly flexible about everything else. My schedule is different every day. The only constant is that it is very full. I'm always rearranging my days to adapt to changes in others' schedules. If the only person who I'm inconveniencing is me, then I will always take that option: "Well, all right. I'll wake up a little earlier. I'll take that red-eye." It's not that I never prioritize myself; I'm just always looking to push the edge in my realm of possible.

  There's one thing in my life that keeps me from pushing it too far: my dog, Lila. If it were just me, I probably wouldn't protect those few moments of quiet that I need every day. But she's another stakeholder, and I'm never going to fail her. She's got to have her leisurely morning walk—preferably somewhere beautiful. (She's picky.) And so I'll always have that time to recharge my batteries.

  Obviously, you don't need a dog to launch a business— but you do need to find a way to hold yourself accountable to recharging your batteries. It can help to recruit others. Get everyone in your life committed to helping you protect that time.

- **Know what you need to stay sane.** From some points of view, it's crazy for me to have a dog. But the truth is she's *exactly* what I need, even down to her breed. I've had a Chow Chow—those big, fluffy dogs Martha Stewart made famous—ever since I launched my first business in Boulder. They're an unusual canine combination of protective but chill. They're super independent, to the point of being too independent for some people, because sometimes they just ignore you. That works for me! I've always been high-strung, and their presence calms me down. They're like little Buddha statues; they find their perch and watch quietly. Having a more active dog might be good for my physical fitness, but it wouldn't be good for my state of mind.

So, I need my Chow Chow. What or who grounds you and makes you feel alive and rewarded? I recommend you generate a list of *healthy* rewards and rituals. Because otherwise you'll go the route of many fine founders and reward yourself by acting out: Accepting one drink too many. Skipping exercise when you know you need it. Falling into a Facebook hole when what really makes you feel good is reading Maya Angelou.

■ **Create rituals.** I hate the word *routine* and am not crazy about *discipline* either. I used to associate routine and the people who require it—to have their morning coffee a certain way or their things arranged just so—as boring and, if I'm honest, intellectually inferior. But I deeply respect *rituals*, the word used by Twyla Tharp in her book *The Creative Habit*, one of my two all-time favorite books for entrepreneurs (more about the second in another hack). And the truth is that unhinged creatives, those sexy badasses, need rituals *the most*. It's how we create the stability we need to *do the work*, or what Twyla calls "face the empty room" with energy, not fear. Where I need Lila, Twyla needs heat. She knows she does her best creative work when she's hot, so she starts every day with enough exercise to get sweaty.

A ritual isn't a "sometimes" kind of thing—it's a regular practice. Finding five minutes to meditate or breathe deeply in a bathroom once things are falling apart isn't what I'm talking about. I'm talking about a practice that happens every single day, including the days where you feel such inner peace (or such lack of time) that you think you might skip it. A daily meditation practice or movement session works for many, but the rituals of the successful (you!) can be wildly idiosyncratic. John Rogers, the founder of Ariel Investments, with more than $12 billion in assets under management, famously spends time almost every day in McDonald's, working through a stack of periodicals. The Golden Arches may not say "sacred ritual space" to everyone, but it's the place that Rogers has chosen to "relax and read and get away from the challenges."[1]

Forget Getting to Yes.
Get to *No*.

"GETTING TO YES" is the premise of a classic book on negotiation. After twenty years in tech—specifically, twenty years as a Latinx in tech—I am an expert at negotiating. I propose that women stop worrying about getting to *yes* and instead switch their attention to *saying no*.

The idea gets tossed around frequently that women are weaker negotiators. And, in fact, a lot of women tell me that they hate negotiating or are bad at it. But whether they know it or not, most women are already experts at exactly what William Ury and Roger Fisher advise to readers in their bestseller: finding win-win agreements. The trouble is, the title of the book perfectly reflects the ass-backward way we've been taught to think about negotiation; it presumes that there is a *no* you're trying to convert into a *yes*. That is, it suggests that someone else has the power in a zero-sum game. I don't know about you, but that feels like a pretty glass-half-empty way of looking at the world. I've spent my career turning *no*s into *yes*es, but the truth is that even when my negotiations led me there, they didn't always take me to success on my terms.

So let's stop negotiating to someone else's *yes* and remember that how we define a skill in relation to ourselves matters. In a 2002 study,[1] a group of men and women were put through a negotiation exercise, divided into two mixed-gender teams. One team was told that the key to succeeding at this exercise was winning at whatever cost, getting what you want, being aggressive, and a litany of other stereotypically "masculine" traits. The other was given a very different pep talk. They were told that the keys to success were to be collaborative, empathetic, and other qualities that are stereotypically "feminine." The result? The women disproportionately underperformed in the first group, and in the second, the women, by a large margin, outperformed their male colleagues. The women who identified themselves in the story of success *were successful*.

And believe me, you already know how to get to *yes*. We all do. We've spent our lives excelling at surviving even when the odds are against us. Meanwhile, women, even those without kids, are burning out and leaving the workforce at a higher rate than men.[2] So here's the hack: Throw out the guides on getting to yes. The most important way to get to success today, on our terms, is getting to *no*. Let's examine all the things we have tacitly accepted as the status quo. We have been saying yes to too much:

- Yes to getting paid less for doing the same jobs as our male colleagues.
- Yes to workplace "asks" such as organizing events that distract us from projects that lead to promotions and power.
- Yes to double standards in the workplace.
- Yes to taking on the majority of the economic and social burden for our families, for our elders, and for our children.
- Yes to doing the majority of the housework when we're in heterosexual partnerships.
- Yes to doing business with companies that don't take care of their workers or the environment.

There's a place at the table for you—so let's collectively agree to say *no* to all the bullshit:

- No to unequal pay.
- No to being the social clerk of our workplaces and our families.
- No to shouldering the majority of the economic burden.
- No to doing all the housework.
- And for goodness sake, *no* to companies that harm workers and the planet.

It's time to fight tooth and nail for the time and focus we need to launch our businesses and put ourselves and our values at the center of our success stories.

MICROHACK

Create a MEL

Feel like you're doing too much at home? Make like tech executive Tiffany Dufu and create a MEL: a Management Excel List spreadsheet that itemizes every task required to keep the household running—and then tracks who in the household is responsible for the task. In her book *Drop the Ball: Achieving More by Doing Less*, Dufu shares how the list helps her and her husband find the most equitable balance of who does what. "The most revealing part of our MEL exercise was deciding which Xs should go in the *No one* column," she writes. "This column represented our acknowledgment that there was more to running our household than both of us could ever accomplish."

Hack 5

Become a Walking Sandwich Board

S o you have a burning idea or a young business. Now: *Who have you told?*

The answer should be *everyone*. If it's not, you're missing out on one of the easiest, cheapest, most effective hacks around. You're not alone. Friends tell me the cool stuff they're doing all the time, then in the next breath say they're keeping their ambitions on the DL, "for now." Let's review the typical excuses:

- What if I don't end up doing it?

   Well, what if? Then you're no worse off than you were. In fact, you're better off, because now people know you're someone with ideas and ambition.
- No way. I don't want anyone stealing the idea.

   Actually, lots of people probably already had the same idea. Idea generators are everywhere. It's executors who are few and far between. So stop worrying and start finding the people who can help. The upsides of spreading the word far outweigh the risks.
- I'm waiting until it's more fully baked.

Every idea is evolving. It's never fully baked. Telling others, getting feedback—positive and negative—is *how* it gets baked.

When I met Nicole Cramer, she was the global chief of staff at McCann Worldgroup—a full-blown New York advertising agency executive, with the stilettos and the worn-out passport and the grueling eighty-hour work week. Despite all this, one of the first things she told me (and never stopped, every time I saw her) was that she was launching a cookie business in rural Pennsylvania on the side. I remember thinking, "Is this legit, or is she dreaming the way I dream of moving to Ecuador and never having to work with a multinational corporation again?"—not seriously, but as a diversion to throw off stress. But whether or not she was serious, I thought it was fun and was impressed by this yearning she had to carry on her grandmother's baking legacy.

Her grandmother, she told me, always had a baked good to offer; it was how she created a safe space of conversation and comfort not just for her family but for the community. Nicole wanted to give others that same gift. Everyone who heard the story left Nicole's side feeling a little happier, from coworkers to friends to her doorman to people she met at parties. And as much as they liked hearing about Nicole's grandma, they were even happier when they saw her basket of cookies appear, as it always did when she had leftovers after a big delivery.

When she started, she baked in her late grandmother's kitchen, a three-and-a-half-hour drive from her apartment in New York. She baked late into the night and got up early to bake a couple of hours more. Then she cooled, packed, loaded up, drove to the delivery, then drove back into Manhattan to work. And while she wasn't telling everyone, "I'm going to leave my job and be a baker," she *was* announcing her plans to open the first brick-and-mortar location and put trucks on the road.

"I thought bringing cookies and conversation to the world

might be a smart endeavor, but I also wanted to bring back this idea of learning from older generations, especially around sharing the experience I had with my own grandmother in learning to bake when I was a very young child," she says.

Today, Nicole, no longer at McCann, is the owner of My Grandma Baked a Cookie Baking Company, with headquarters in Pocono Lake, Pennsylvania. She chose the locale for better proximity to New York than her grandmother's home and because the business ultimately required a commercial kitchen. She employs two bakers in Pennsylvania and a third at a second location in Vermont, fulfilling a long-time vision of creating jobs. The company has also expanded to an online storefront. She has projected profitability a year out from that opening. In the meantime, she supports herself with a consulting company, trading on the skills she developed in more than fifteen years in global marketing and operations.

The Walking Sandwich Board hack played a major role in Nicole's journey. She made a conscious effort to put herself out there from the beginning, boldly and fearlessly, for three reasons. First, voicing your intention makes your plan clearer not just to others but to yourself. "It's one thing to say it in your mind or write it in your journal, but it's another thing to actually give voice to it in front of other people, because once you hear it said in your own voice, it takes on a completely different meaning," she says. "Sometimes it makes you go, 'Oh my god, that . . . No. Why would I ever do that?' But mostly it hopefully makes you go, 'Yes, that's exactly what my intention is.'"

Second, sharing your business plans encourages people to see you in a new light. It's a natural instinct to pigeonhole. If you're an ad exec, you're one thing. If you're a cashier, you're another. Understanding something new about your personality expands how people think they can interact with you and in some cases raises your status. A lightbulb goes off in people's heads: "Oh, this person is more than X. Interesting."

Third and most important, that lightbulb can lead to a slew of opportunities. You probably don't know your future first clients personally, and especially not your first big clients. Your circle is too small. But your circle's circle? That's much, much wider. "Hopefully you have a network like mine where people started thinking, 'I want to buy cookies. I want to tell my friends. Who could I introduce her to?'" she says. For example, Nicole is an active alumna volunteer at Cornell University and sits on the President's Council of Cornell Women. One day she was casually chatting with another board member about her burgeoning cookie business. That woman, it turned out, ran a volunteer program, and eventually hired My Grandma Baked a Cookie to supply their events. Nicole stresses that the people she's told who have been the most helpful often haven't been the ones who are highly placed or influential—it's been the people who have *cared* the most. "It doesn't matter if your network is fifty janitors or one global CEO," she says. "At the end of the day, having the fifty janitors in your network can actually be more beneficial than having the one CEO—if those janitors know you, love you, and are willing to talk to people on your behalf."

But speak up: You're going to have to tell them first.

Hack Your Inner "Peer" Circle

To LEAPFROG TO success, you need a peer circle—people to hold you accountable, people to pick you up when you're down, people to see who you are, believe in you, and keep you moving. But first you need to rip apart your old idea of what a peer is and how you find one. The people who can support you through the entrepreneur's journey likely aren't at arm's reach—so you have to work harder to find them.

I learned this in late summer 2005 in Seattle. I was struggling. I had stepped down recently from Bowne Global Solutions to partner with Lionbridge, a global translation company. Not long after coming on board, we made a plan to acquire BGS, the company that I had helped grow. It was not a friendly takeover, and as the stress increased, my confidence plummeted.

I was having massive imposter syndrome. Why did anyone think I could lead in our new, merged reality? Yes, I had been successful at BGS. But all my past successes had been anchored to my specialty, tech globalization. In this new role, I couldn't rely solely on that. I was now dealing with lawyers, antitrust issues, mergers and acquisitions—all stuff I had never experienced before.

My peers at the time were mostly men. I also had plenty of male mentors, guys working on a track similar to mine or clients invested in my success. They were really good at teaching me the basic skills of business. The trouble was that they would never be able to advise me about this fear that was waking me up at four o'clock in the morning, giving me agita: that I was a fraud. These colleagues and mentors didn't seem to have a problem feeling their way through new responsibilities with confidence. And they certainly didn't have to face the pressure of being the only woman in the room in the tensest of situations.

Into this anxious period of my life walked Awilda Verdejo, a woman who redefined my understanding of the kinds of people I needed to pull in close if I wanted to keep moving forward fast. In fact, she changed my approach to business forever. She was a specialist herself: a semiretired Nuyorican opera singer. I met her at a women's networking dinner after she elbowed her way up next to me and announced to the group, "The only reason I'm here at this dinner is to meet *this* young woman"—ME!—"so if you don't mind, I'd like to sit next to her."

She went on to become one of my most important advisors—despite not knowing an M&A from an M&M. When I told Awilda I felt like a fraud, she gave me the answer I needed. She rejected the idea that I wasn't ready for the work I was doing. "*You* are the source of your own supply," she told me. Today those words are my mantra, but it took her sustained support and counsel, along with that of an entire group of women I began to call upon in Seattle, to get me to truly believe it. These were women I had met at events, parties, anywhere, really. It was a wildly diverse group. I sought out peers along two parameters: One, they were driven like me, and two, they also needed support from other women fighting seemingly impossible battles. Awilda had proven to me that the "peers" who could help me most weren't necessarily my work colleagues or even in my field.

With the help of my new circle, my confidence even in

unfamiliar territory began to grow, along with my willingness to step into authority. A turning point came when I was leading a massive expansion and ran into a problem with an HR manager in Copenhagen. He had sent me a list of candidates to manage the Scandinavian arm of our business. Most of the people were fairly junior for the role, but one stood out as well qualified: a former Microsoft employee from Finland named Helena Kemppainen.

When I told the HR manager that she was my choice, he balked. "No one will accept a female leader from Finland!" he said, explaining that Finns are basically regarded as second-class citizens within Scandinavia.

After weeks of back-and-forth in email, I was getting nowhere. My male mentors wouldn't have known how to coach me. Tactics that had worked for them, with their booming voices and towering height, might not serve me so well. Trying to follow them would only make me less confident and able to tap my own power. So I called on my posse, who patiently listened to me vent and each shared their stories of how they had dealt with difficult people, and, let's face it, difficult men, specifically. They urged me not to back down. Lifted up by their strength, I steeled myself and flew to Copenhagen.

I arrived at his office for an eleven o'clock meeting. The entire staff listened at the door while this man screamed at me. His arguments rocketed from rational to completely racist. (At one point he screamed, "Finns are a people without *literature*!")

There were moments when I might have said to myself, "This isn't worth the effort," and asked for a stack of new résumés. But when my resolve weakened, I thought of my circle and I thought of Helena. I was doing this for her and for all women. (And all Finns!) My experience with my pals in Seattle had given me a profound sense of *solidarity*.

So throughout the crazy, I sat calmly. He kept saying, "What do you have to say?" And I kept answering, "I don't have anything to say. You know my decision. It's mine to make. If you want to continue yelling about it, that's fine by me." So he just kept yelling. Until 11:59 a.m., when I gathered up my stuff and left with a nod.

Within days, he announced to the company that Helena Kemppainen was my team's new Scandinavian regional manager. Business went on as usual, and she thrived in the role.

Faced with someone screaming at me for an hour, in a foreign culture, in his office, on his turf, I had not backed down. That hour gave me a lifetime of confidence, and to this day I don't believe I could have stood my ground if my circle of peers hadn't given me the fortitude to walk into that room and stand up for a woman I had never met.

Ten years later, I was sitting in the office of the Athena Center for Leadership Studies on Barnard's campus, chatting with Lulu Mickelson, who was then a student but also a civic entrepreneur, as she put it. She was hard at work founding Columbia's chapter of Design for America, a nationwide network of interdisciplinary student teams and community members using design thinking to create local and social impact. Lulu was feeling lonely in her work. She said she wished she had more peers to talk to about building her organization. She didn't like to bother "regular" friends with it, and anyway, they could listen but didn't have much to contribute.

Something clicked for me: Peers are typically the people who life throws us together with—fellow students, colleagues, etc. But when you become an entrepreneur, you have to hack peerdom. You need to find the people who are facing similar challenges and redefine the notion of *peer* around your entrepreneurship.

Everyone launching a business needs a peer group, but leapfroggers, swimming upstream against institutional and cultural currents, need one even more. These relationships might be informal or formal, as in an organized group that meets with a certain frequency over a certain period. Either way, you'll always need that caliber of support and accountability, people you can call anytime to give you *the talk*—to sustain your belief and your action in those moments when you start to feel like a fraud or like you can't make it. Accountability is so important in the early stages of entrepreneurship, so full of unknowns, self-doubt, and, in many unfortunate cases, loneliness.

And either way, you can't trust it to happen naturally. You have to define and find these peers, which suggests some level of formality from the get-go. You might even find that a formal circle is also particularly helpful to support and propel a big push in your business—whether that's launching, getting a round of investment, or scaling up.

So, who are your peers in your new endeavor? Women—and all leapfroggers, regardless of gender—launching different kinds of businesses, are united first and foremost by their fiery pursuit of their goals. Most important, you need people who can identify with and support you through the emotional challenges of launching a business. What those people look like will vary. For example, if you're a mom wondering how you're going to fit everything in, you might consider allying with other caretakers who understand the special challenges of launching while shouldering family responsibilities. You could even make shared babysitting, either by swapping kids or going in together on a paid sitter, part of your approach to getting things done.

But here's the thing: The whole point is that by starting a business, you are doing something unique. You can't rely on serendipity to bring you a network or assume that your lifelong best friend will know how to support you. (That doesn't mean she's not important—these new peers are an "and" not an "or.") Use every tool available to find them: Facebook, LinkedIn, your school, your mosque, your neighborhood bulletin board, your chamber of commerce—these are all places to recruit. There are also a number of organizations and businesses that exist solely to connect and support women entrepreneurs, such as Dreamers // Doers, SheWorx, the Collective (of Us), Women Who Tech, and Black Female Founders (#BFF).

Once you find your new peers, consider creating a formal "mastermind" group—a group that meets regularly to create action items and hold one another to them. Four questions to answer up front:

1. How long will members commit to participating? At Athena, our program ran for nine months, which mirrored the school year but also felt like the right term to "birth" something big.
2. How often will you meet, and where? We met monthly, a frequency that wasn't onerous but kept the group top of mind.
3. What prerequisites will there be—for example, should they have a specific goal they are working to accomplish or have already reached a common milestone? At Athena, they had to be launching or have recently launched their startup.
4. What will happen at meetings? We always met over a meal and had just one agenda (beyond enjoyment): Everyone at the table had to commit to three to four measurable action items and share progress on the previous month's.

The Athena Mastermind groups changed my life and the lives of the other women in them. I wouldn't want to launch a business without a mastermind to lean on, and if I were you or anyone not interested in running in circles, I wouldn't either.

Hack 7

Steal Paper Clips

CHANCES ARE YOU'RE starting your business as a side hustle. Right: You need a way to bring in money while you invest in your business. You can give yourself a big leg up if you can find or reshape your day job so that it is contributing to the future you want to create, beyond your paycheck. What resources are available to you there? Don't actually steal paper clips, but look for honest perks. Is it a source of contacts, training, support, or clientele? Can you use it to build the influence and reputation that pave the way to your own business? If not, maybe it's time to find a job that's a better fit for your future.

My friend and former mastermind partner Elise Schuster drafted off her day job—actually, multiple day jobs—to start Okayso, a company that will deliver sex ed to teens through a mobile app that won't embarrass them, patronize them, or leave them wondering. (Elise is one of many tech founders I know with no tech background. Don't let that stop you.)

She and her cofounder, Francisco, came up with the idea for the app while working on one of his freelance projects. It was 2011, and he had been hired to produce content for a sex-ed TV show. Because Elise had worked for years as an educator and workshop leader for the sex-positive toy shop Babeland, he called in his friend to help. The TV show was great, but what about an *app* for sex ed? they thought. Had anyone ever done one?

All they could find in their research were tacky novelty apps—nothing like the safe, validating experiences Elise gave people while teaching for Babeland. "These apps were all quizzes and sex tips and facts. All the graphics were like satin and silhouetted ladies," she says. "It was so gross, like walking into an Eighth Avenue sex-toy shop." To Elise, sex education is about so much more than sex, a topic I love to hear her riff on passionately. "Sex is a microcosm of people's lives. I get to help them to develop things like a sense of their right to have needs, or just to exist in the world, and to communicate better in all aspects of their lives," she says.

Around that time, Elise had moved on from Babeland and was working at a New York City–based youth-development agency that helps young people with problems like homelessness and abuse. She was building the agency a training institute, which included writing the curriculum. Since she already had similar experience at Babeland, she had the equivalent of years of on-the-job training to write the curriculum that would drive Okayso.

Training is one major potential benefit of a day gig. Here are four other smart ways you can profit from the right day job:

1. **Insider knowledge:** Intimate knowledge of an industry from the inside allows you to spot opportunities and dream up solutions more easily than someone who has experienced a space only as a customer. Thanks to years at Babeland, Elise understood exactly how underserved people are by most sex education. She also understood the questions behind the questions that surface during discussions about sex.

2. **Access to customers:** If your day job gives you access to the kind of people you'll eventually call customers, you can do market research for your future business just by doing your

job. Many clients at her youth development job were in the target age range for Elise's app, so while she and Francisco were prototyping, she pulled together a handful to ask what they'd want in an app.

3. **Network:** Already having a strong network of relationships in your business's space is invaluable. When Elise set out to attract sex experts to answer users' questions in the app, many of her early "gets" were Babeland folks whom she'd stayed in touch with over the years.

4. **Future marketing or distribution partners:** If your business complements rather than competes with your employer's, they could be natural marketing or distribution partners down the line. Elise hopes that some of the health service providers connected to the youth development agency, for example, might be willing to recommend the app to patients. And while it may be too early to ask, Babeland seems like a natural conduit for spreading the news when the app is available to the public.

Elise and her CTO, Will Luxion, are barreling forward with Okayso. (Francisco has since left the company.) After getting turned down by Y Combinator's tech incubator program, the pair ended up with a major win: In 2016, they received a $322,000 grant *without giving away any equity*. That's a hack in itself! They won a contest sponsored by a federally funded national nonprofit called Power to Decide. It's enough cash to get their app from prototype to minimum viable product—in other words, the earliest, most basic version of their app that they're comfortable sharing with investors and early beta testers. They're the only contest winners who are incorporated as a for-profit, not a nonprofit—but Elise says that whatever the business model, they'll always offer free access to the kind of basic sex ed that can save lives.

Hack 8

The DIY Business School

B E SMART: HACK your education. Order a la carte, or off the menu entirely. Don't be constrained by what everybody else does or what's expected. Take a laser-focused inventory of what *you* need, then design the educational opportunity to make it happen.

I mentioned earlier that I dropped out of college to launch my first business. Nearly two decades later, I decided to go back to school. But I didn't do what most people expected, which was to get an Executive MBA. Instead, I went to theater school. To study playwriting. As a full-time student.

At first, I considered getting an MBA to encourage and sharpen the skills that had already served me, especially storytelling—my secret sauce. I looked at programs focused on marketing and branding, because fundamentally that's what storytelling is. But everywhere I looked, the people teaching the classes were similar in age and experience level to myself. I felt as though they'd just give me more of the same. I realized that going to business people to hone my storytelling prowess was the wrong idea. The real experts lived elsewhere. And so I turned my attention to the arts, picked Columbia, and spent two years writing, staging plays, and going to the theater as homework. My time there fundamentally changed how I communicate today and differentiates me from everyone else. Equally important, it filled my creative cup, which had been drained by many years spent deep in the world of tech.

Now, am I saying that more typical higher ed has nothing to offer? Is an MBA worthless? No way. Education is one of history's most reliable leapfrogs for outsiders, giving them an immediate patina of credibility. In a world where anyone can have a Gucci bag, education has become an even higher-ticket status symbol. Since 1996, the top 1 percent of earners have tripled what they spend on education, while they've been spending less and less on material goods.[1] Anyone who gets in and can find a way to foot tuition (good luck) can learn and earn cultural capital—those signals that you are *in the tribe*.

So if you're young and have time to spend four years at school, by all means, shoot for the moon and seek out the assistance and opportunities out there. But if you've passed the point when you can add a name-brand university to your résumé, don't stress. Plenty of people without high-end educational backgrounds have launched successful businesses. Girlboss Sophia Amoruso (community college dropout), Sara Blakely of Spanx (Florida State), and Oprah (Tennessee State dropout) all come to mind.

Here's the thing to remember: There's credibility, and there's *learning*. These are related but separate. When entrepreneurs need to close their own knowledge gaps, what they often find is that they can't do it with an existing curriculum. The knowledge needed is either too new or too specific.

An entrepreneur's educational journey is completely bespoke: custom-tailored and powered by ingenuity and audacity. Take Tanya Menendez, who had a mission to increase access to technology and education among low-income workers. When she first thought about what she needed to serve her target audience, she realized that it had been many years since she'd worked a blue-collar job—so she applied for one. She spent the next few weeks in a grocery store doing backbreaking work like mopping floors, working the register, and stocking shelves. She could never build a tool for hourly wage workers without understanding exactly what they were facing every day.

Tanya's entire career has been in alternative education, helping nontraditional students meet needs that aren't being served by traditional pathways. Her last company, Maker's Row, helps designers find U.S. manufacturers and access online training about how to work with them. Her experience there gave her the idea for her next business, Metas, which is focused on serving first-generation American students with a platform providing them everything from training and mentorship to job placement.

Tanya herself is a first-generation student. She went to the University of San Diego and finished a sociology degree in three years while working forty hours a week to support herself. "Even if you have a four-year degree these days, you don't really have the language and the playbook to get the type of job that will allow you to earn a living wage," she says. She offers two things that she thinks can help leapfroggers get the most out of wherever their education takes them:

1. **Intentionality:** She's an advocate of the four-year-degree program. As the child of immigrants—her parents are from Nicaragua and El Salvador—she also knows from her own experience that cultural education can be as important as book learning. But she stresses the importance of being intentional every step of the way, from picking your professors to courses to a major to the clubs you join. You can't do it just to do it; you have to take advantage of every opportunity. She also recommends working while you're a student, so that you finish with job experience already on your résumé.

2. **Curiosity:** If you're going to start a company, you won't get far if you're not willing to ask a lot of questions. "Probably

some people wouldn't have taken a cashier job because they don't want to have to mop a floor when they have a college degree. But I think you have to put your ego aside in order to fulfill your curiosity and make sure you know everything about what you're doing. Be open to learning from anyone," Tanya advises.

The bottom line is, it's up to you to customize your education. There's no product that's out there that's going to help you do exactly what you need. Besides, the art of leapfrogging is about getting *better* results than everyone else. Use a cookie cutter for your education and you're likely to get the same cookies.

Aside from seriously assessing what you need and where to find it, I'm a big believer in creating informal, short-term apprenticeships with people who are working in a space where you need knowledge. If there's something that you think is going to be important to your business, figure out a way to step into that world and learn firsthand. So, for example, if you're looking to build technology to help pilots, ask a private flying instructor if you can listen in as she trains students in the classroom and in the sky.

No one is going to walk up to you with an acceptance letter and a curriculum for the business you're launching. Be assertive in doing the research, knocking on doors, and building the relationships to *create* the learning experience you need.

Cash in on Your Woman Card

You, WOMAN ENTREPRENEUR, have a responsibility to do everything in your power to succeed—including tapping into the hidden, unused funding that is there to support you. Many corporations and government agencies have a mandate to prioritize diversity when they seek vendors, suppliers, and partners, but most of us have no idea these programs exist. So scour the internet for opportunities, contests, and programs that are specifically for women and underrepresented groups.

I personally pulled the woman card to get Barnard College an expedited license for TEDxWomen. Their website clearly states it takes six to eight weeks to process an application, longer than we could wait. I saw that the New York region was packed with TEDx events, but not one for TEDxWomen, the annual TED offshoot focused on the power of women and girls. And I saw that there were very few women's colleges that had been given TEDx licenses. Bingo. I presented the facts, and we had our TEDxBarnardCollege license in twenty-four hours.

Recently, I met Rosa Santana, a businesswoman from El Paso, Texas, who several years ago made an incredible leapfrog, with a heap of hard work. Rosa founded a small temp agency, Integrated

Human Capital (IHC), after several years as a leading executive in the staffing industry. To differentiate her new company, she got it certified as woman- and minority-owned. As the company grew, she opened an office in San Antonio because she learned that Toyota was opening a facility there. When a supplier to Toyota needed a cleaning crew to prepare the construction site, IHC got the contract. Rosa's team exceeded expectations, leading to many other opportunities with the supplier.

Fast-forward through ten dedicated years of incredible service and relationship building, and IHC had become Toyota's supplier of choice. And so it was Rosa who the company turned to when it was time to solve a new problem. Executives wanted to outsource the assembly of the Tacoma pickup's truck bed, and they wanted their new outsourcing partner to be a certified minority-owned business. But such manufacturing businesses are still few and far between. They knew Rosa's expertise was in hiring people and building teams, but they also knew the relationship they had built over time. She could run a business that delivered excellence; the rest they were willing to teach her.

Toyota committed to helping Rosa expand her existing business to become their new assembly partner. They even loaned her an executive whose sole purpose was to help Rosa succeed. In 2014, Forma Automotive was founded, becoming Toyota's first Hispanic, woman-owned direct Tier One supplier. Today Rosa isn't just the owner of a small temp agency; she's the founder and CEO of Santana Group, which is five companies strong. Rosa is a regional leader in both staffing *and* manufacturing, and she runs her businesses with the help of her two daughters.

Were there other manufacturing companies that were better prepared out of the gate to take on Toyota's business? Sure. But Rosa had proven herself to be a worthy business partner. Toyota had priorities that ranked as high as manufacturing experience, and Rosa met all their needs. No diversity program is ever a free ride. Rosa earned every opportunity, even as certification opened new doors.

So don't hesitate to get yourself certified, especially if you are looking to partner with large corporations and government agencies, which are more likely to have formal diversity mandates. There are a bunch of options, both regional and national: Start with the Women's Business Enterprise National Council (WBENC), the Small Business Administration's 8(a) program, and the National Minority Supplier Development Council. I'll be real: You'll be filling out a lot of paperwork, it can take months to process, and certification can cost a few hundred dollars or more. But once you've invested, you open up countless doors for your business and become eligible for a wealth of opportunities.

For Athenia Rodney, the CEO of Umoja Events & Decor, whose company was recently certified as a minority- and woman-owned business enterprise (MWBE) in New York, networking has been the big win. She decided to apply after several corporate clients told her that certification would allow them to use her company for bigger projects. "We do get invited to more networking events," she says. "The MTA invited us to one. We stood up and said what our business was and had the chance to meet all the different agencies." Nina Vaca, the CEO of workforce solutions provider Pinnacle Group, agrees that the real benefit isn't the certification itself but the networking opportunities it provides; she got her first major corporate client thanks to an introduction from WBENC.

The downside? As I mentioned, the application process is no joke; Athenia estimates she spent eighty to one hundred hours hunting down documents, working with employees to add detail to their résumés, and asking her accountant to adjust how they were running profit and loss statements to the required format.

"You can apply on your own like I did, but I don't advise it," says Athenia. "I didn't pay anyone to help me, but time is money." She did get free help from some of the many government agencies that exist to support small businesses, such as the SBA. Next she's going to apply to the federal program so that she'll become eligible for military contracts.

Certification is only the tip of the iceberg of programs to support women entrepreneurs. Nely Galán has assembled a compendium of these opportunities at becomingselfmade.com, and new ones are added all the time.

Cashing in on your woman card means embracing arrogance. Arrogance is an entrepreneur's friend. Being part of a diversity program doesn't make you any less qualified than the white dude the next office over. It makes you scrappy. It makes you ambitious and determined. I promise you that *every* successful person out there has taken a shortcut—and didn't get angsty about whether they were worthy. If Lady Gaga (or any other pop star, for that matter) had used a checklist to compare herself to her competition, she might still be living in her Lower East Side tenement wondering what to do with her life. Of course she'd find somewhere that she fell short. You know your unique strengths and purpose. You know you earned every opportunity extended to you. So don't worry a minute about what anyone else thinks.

Reframe it this way: You have a *responsibility* not just to take help when it's offered but to find and follow every ethical shortcut you can. Otherwise you're wasting time and money. There are so few women at the top and even fewer women of color. You're not just striving for yourself; you're striving for everyone who will come after you. You're wasting their time *if you don't* cash in your woman card!

Hack 10

Worry About Success, Not Failure

I'VE NOTICED THAT people love to think about what will happen if they fail. In a weird way it's safer, clearer territory than what they really *need* to be thinking about—what will happen if they succeed. It's like they don't dare go there. But if you don't plan for the best-case scenario, success can become the worst thing that ever happened to you, like the lottery winner who ends up bankrupt because she quickly outspends her winnings. You could end up in a life that's an uncomfortable match for your values or lifestyle.

Ask yourself: Are you building toward an endgame that will truly make you happy?

When you're working hard to start a business, it's easy to be so consumed with the hustle—with what the product or the customer needs, or just with the race to win—that you don't stop to think about what you really need or want. I almost buried this hack in the back of the book, but then I realized it's a critical early step. The truth is that if you can be clear on what you want up front, you can make serious decisions about what you're building and how—decisions better made sooner than later.

Xochi Birch is the cofounder of a hugely successful private club in San Francisco. In 2014, *The New York Times* described the Battery as "a 58,000-square-foot, five-bar, five-story house of mirth."[1] It's a cultural hub and a thriving business, because Xochi and her husband have fine-tuned every aspect of the experience. Once their reputation spread, people naturally started asking, "What's next, London? LA? New York?" Xochi surprised them all by opting for "none of the above." She knew that expanding locations would have been the most obvious way to trade on what they had achieved. But when she played out what it would look like, she didn't like what she saw: moving to city after city and getting to know them well enough to get everything right—a major investment of time and energy. Meanwhile, she has two school-age kids (and a third in college) whom she didn't want to uproot. So she resisted the pressure. "It might just be the technology industry, where you always hear about the big successes, but it feels like there's either zero or one hundred and nothing in between. For you to be successful, you have to go to one hundred," she says. "Rightly or wrongly, my family life dictates how I choose to spend my time." But success isn't actually zero-sum. Xochi realized there were ways to both grow the business and allow her family to maintain the life they enjoy.

Here's the thing about Xochi. A couple of decades ago, she and her husband were scrappy web developers who mortgaged their house to bootstrap and build several early web businesses. One, BirthdayAlarm, immediately became a solid revenue generator that supported their other efforts, which eventually included the creation of a social networking site. That was Bebo, which they sold to AOL in 2008 for hundreds of millions of dollars.

Point is, Xochi, the hard-working, lucky lady that she is, can chew on these questions of meaning from a position of complete financial independence. Most of us are so hungry for financial security that we shove more qualitative, personal issues under the rug—so much so that it's damn hard to find examples of people who planned smart from day 1. But I promise, if you don't get really intentional about what kind of life you want, it eventually catches up with you.

In the first half of my career, I took each opportunity as it came. Where that landed me was managing a huge team in a multinational company. I wasn't bad at it—um, depending on which 50 percent of my direct reports you asked—but I really didn't like it. I didn't like having hundreds of people who I barely knew working for me. I was burning out quickly. If I had thought early on about what kind of business would be the best fit for the life I wanted, I might have invested in a franchise, grown to a few locations, and been a little happier and a lot less stressed. Other people would be running my businesses while I split my time between lobbying Congress for women's rights and chilling in Ecuador.

My decision to found BRAVA was first and foremost born from a sense of urgency to make a bigger impact—but it is also in alignment with my professional and personal preferences. If we're doing things right, we can be managing billions of dollars with a handful of staff. I can have a few deep, collaborative relationships *and* touch millions through our platform and through the work of the companies we invest in.

I've helped several women entrepreneurs I mentor create space for answering some of these questions by leading them through this meditation. I ask them to close their eyes. "Imagine all the things that you wish were true," I say. "Imagine you've not just launched your business but seen it become wildly successful beyond anything you could have imagined. You've achieved your dreams. Now, in this world you have created, picture yourself waking up in the morning." Then I ask them to walk me through a whole day—not a perfect day of today or tomorrow but one in the world where their dreams have come true—by asking a series of questions: *What are you having for breakfast? Is somebody with you in bed? Where are you waking up? Are you on a tropical island? Are you in the middle of Manhattan? Do you have kids? What's the first thing you're going to do? Are you going to go to an office or not?*

When we're done, we look at their dream day and the business they're building and can usually see pretty quickly if they can coexist. Someone might tell me she wants to live a quiet life on a ranch in Montana—but meanwhile is building a business like Martha Stewart, where she's the center of the brand and could never walk away. Someone else might tell me they want to be married but has a business that requires them to travel 280 days a year.

Now you might say, "Can't I build a business and then exit so I can afford my actual dream life on an island?" That may well happen, but I believe that you've got to love the journey. Business is often a war of attrition. The winners are the last ones standing. You need a plan that's at least somewhat in balance with your values and lifestyle if you're going to survive the startup years.

Find a way to align your ambitions with the lifestyle you want. Xochi and her husband did. They're going back to their roots, building software to help the hospitality industry do a better job with customer management. It allows Xochi to do what she loves most—nurture an early-stage business—without moving out of town.

Give the meditation a try. Commit your perfect day to paper, and keep it close at hand as you make the big decisions. Not every single decision you make will map directly to your "perfect world," but at least you'll know what it looks like and let it influence how you build every step closer to the dream.

Set

Read about startup life and you'll see a lot of talk about *pivoting.* Throw something at the wall, the thinking goes, and see if it sticks; if not, pivot. While I'm all for iterative product development, as general business advice this is better suited to someone burning through a million or two in VC funding than someone dumping out their proverbial piggy bank. Smart planning and thoughtfulness can help get you to sustainable revenue and profitability more quickly. In other words, when you're lean on cash, you can't afford to have too many rough drafts. You've got to be scrappier than most. The hacks in this section will help you go beyond getting ready and into developing a smart idea and a sustainable business that is designed to scale.

Forget Passion. Find Things You Want to Punch.

I spent four years at Barnard teaching and encouraging women to consider entrepreneurship, and in 2017, I zigzagged around the country, co-leading the entrepreneurship track of Galvanize, the United State of Women's weekend-long training boot camp. What I've learned is that almost everyone is scared of the same two things.

The first is leaving behind a steady paycheck. Understandable, particularly if you have little ones depending on you. There are lots of ways to make that transition easier—the side hustle, grants, scholarships, etc. But making the numbers work takes time and planning, and for most people, it doesn't stop being scary for a long, long time.

The second fear is internal. People worry that they don't have good enough ideas, or the "vision," to start a business. I've figured out how to banish that fear in ten minutes with one simple exercise. So, stop reading, right now, and make a list of ten things you want to punch. Ten problems in your daily life, small or large, that are making you frown, cry, or want to raise hell. Do it whether you identify with this particular fear or not—it's useful either way. Go ahead; I'll be right here when you get back.

Hi! You're back. You're a woman trying to make your way in this world; don't *tell* me you didn't find ten things! Repeat this exercise every day, and I guarantee you'll develop at least a few amazing business ideas. All you really need is to be constantly on the lookout for PITAs—*pains in the ass* that need solving, especially those you see lots of other people struggling with, too.

Maybe you've heard the word *ideation* get tossed around and aren't quite sure what it means. Well, it's exactly that—coming up with business ideas—no technical language or MBA necessary. Two more words that can intimidate and confuse are *vision* and *passion*. You don't have to have your eye on interstellar travel or world peace to make a solid, scalable business. And we're all passionate about plenty, but funneling those passions into a business isn't always easy. But things we want to punch? Bring it on! Launching a business is infinitely easier if you know personally what needs fixing. Sometimes the best ideas don't need much vision at all. They're right in your own backyard.

Adda Birnir never thought of herself as someone who would or could "ideate" (gag), let alone run, a business. Adda studied art and African American studies at Yale with plans to be an artist and journalist. She graduated and got a great job producing content for an online magazine. Amid a big round of layoffs, she jumped ship to another great content job—and got laid off herself. She looked around her industry: Editorial and creative professionals were struggling. It didn't matter whether you had a Yale degree. If writing was your bag, you were disposable.

Adda had found something she wanted to punch. She also saw a solution.

Guess who wasn't getting laid off? People with technical skills, like basic web development. So she said screw it and taught herself to code. She bought a book, went to friends for guidance, and basically banged her head against her computer until things started working. Soon she was getting freelance work, and then she used that to transition into a full-time technical position. That year, she made more money than she would have if she hadn't been laid off.

She realized that there were plenty of other creatives out there who could make themselves more valuable if they added tech to their résumés. But when she suggested her path to others, they told her it was too hard, too outside their skill set. From there, her business was born: Skillcrush, an online educational platform targeted specifically to this demographic's needs, skills, and concerns. Adda was her own best success story, and the perfect person to teach others how.

Of course, it wasn't easy. Like many entrepreneurs, she didn't start her business with all the skills she'd need to make it successful. When I met her a few years back in our mastermind group, she was working on buttoning up Skillcrush's finances and stepping up her promotional game. Since then, she's expanded to thirty-five employees, has a newsletter audience of more than 250,000, and is approaching $3 million in annual revenue.

Be like Adda, and follow the money. What's making your life difficult? Fix it. Crack open your creativity by starting from the impossible and working backward. I've watched hundreds of women do this exercise—and create more than a few brilliant business ideas. A group of students at my summer camp wanted a "magical" trash can for neighborhood streets that could empty itself (the thing they wanted to punch in the face was overflowing cans littering their local streets). That "impossible" idea ultimately led them to a beautifully designed trash can with an LED screen that they could sell advertising on, which would provide the funding for more frequent upkeep—a great sustainable business idea. Even more brilliant was the name they gave it: "Pretty Trashy."

Your turn: Take the list you wrote just now, and come up with three outrageous solutions for each thing you wanted to punch. Let your thinking be magical. That's ultimately what ideation is all about.

Hack 12

A Closed Network Is Open Season

IT'S A LOT easier to leapfrog if you've got a product that you can market to a closed network—a tight, high-trust community where everyone knows everyone and information spreads quickly. You'll barely need to market your product, if it's any good; word of mouth will do the job for you. The most famous example in the field is Mark Zuckerberg. When he launched "The Facebook" at Harvard, it took only twelve hours to get twelve hundred students with profiles and only a month to get half of the *entire student body*. University after university, adoption came at the speed of light because students shared it with friends, who signed up and passed word along as well.

One company I love is BeautyLynk, which has flourished in large part thanks to the devoted network its founder built and then marketed to. I met its awesome founder, Modjossorica (Rica) Elysée, at the Women Entrepreneurs Boot Camp co-created by my friend Lynn Loacker at the Davis Wright Tremaine law firm. The company got its start as a platform for on-demand styling services for women with natural black hair. Rica had started a local Meetup group for black women who were throwing out their hair relaxers (and, with them, racist cultural norms) and celebrating their beautiful natural hair. The group grew to twelve hundred local members and an online community of twenty-five thousand, which became the perfect source for Rica to create a network of stylists who specialized in their needs. Rica has since expanded to include all hair types and ethnicities, and BeautyLynk is in sixty cities, with fourteen thousand beauty professionals on call. In 2016, she won $50,000 in prize money as a Gold winner in the MassChallenge accelerator program—her first infusion of outside capital. But without question, her early traction came from serving a high-trust community—one that she had helped grow. "I built my trust system, and I love the people I'm serving and the team I've built," says Rica.

To find a network's unmet need, listen when people complain, and pay attention for possible gaps you can help fill. My friend Roberta Pereira is a successful theater producer in New York. She was having drinks with a friend one day when they hit her with a question she had never considered: "Why is no one publishing novels about Broadway? Where is our *Devil Wears Prada?*" Here was a niche market that was under the radar of big publishers, yet hungry for fiction set in their world. And so Roberta and her friend decided to be the first and launched Dress Circle Publishing. Word traveled fast in the small, chatty world of Broadway, making their titles an instant smash. Now, according to *Forbes*, Dress Circle is a "profitable enterprise with multiple best-sellers under its auspices, a ravenous fanbase, and at least one television spin-off in the works."[1]

A few more examples of closed networks:

- Neighborhood groups and associations
- PTAs and parent groups
- Religious communities
- Alumnae groups (particularly local outposts)
- Interest-driven communities, like sports clubs or hobbyists

As you think about going to market, take careful inventory of the networks in your own life and community. Which of them might be down with your business? You don't necessarily need to be a member to approach these groups, if you can offer them a good deal on something they really need. When Leah Busque launched her business TaskRabbit, for example, she knew she needed a high-trust user base to test what was then a kooky idea: paying neighbors to run your errands. She found a mothers' organization in her neighborhood with six hundred members. She wasn't a mom herself, but she knew that they were people who could really use an extra set of hands. Soon the moms in that first neighborhood were spreading the word to moms in other neighborhoods, and the company was off and running. In 2017, IKEA bought Leah's company, having figured out that a lot of people (me, for example) can't put together a PAX wardrobe to save their lives. What is now a global business all started with a tight-knit, chatty group of six hundred moms in Boston.

Let the Techies Tech

Tech almost always brings a leapfrog effect. Incorporate it into your business model, and you dramatically increase your chances of scaling and attracting customers. You don't need to be a coder to make it happen.

Just recently I met the perfect example of a non-techie who made that kind of leap. John Henry is a partner at Harlem's only venture capital firm, Harlem Capital. He's a twenty-four-year-old black Latinx millionaire, a kid whose immigrant parents earned a combined $25,000 a year. But unlike most young VCs, he didn't get where he is by cashing out as an early employee of Google or Facebook, or because he knew someone who would give him $5 million for an idea on the back of a napkin.

John Henry became a hot tech entrepreneur . . . by starting a dry-cleaning delivery service. He built a simple service business with word of mouth and hustle, using his day job as a doorman to find top-dollar customers. He grew it into a profitable business and expanded into pet care and housekeeping. At that point, it wasn't the kind of high-growth opportunity that would lead most investors to look twice. But John didn't stop there: He reinvested in the company by hiring a buddy to build an app that allowed customers to order the services he offered on demand. Off the heat of the app, one of his vendors offered to acquire him, making him a millionaire at twenty-one.

John was doing great without tech. But once he added it, he entered a different stratosphere of power and influence—which meant being able to contribute to his community at a scale beyond what he could ever do with his offline business.

Being slow to embrace new technology can get you into trouble. Be relentless in picking apart your business, from scheduling to marketing to customer service, to see where an existing application could add value or help you find and serve new customers. When I met Modjossorica Elysée, the founder of BeautyLynk, she told me, "In two years, we'll have a mobile app." I told her, "You need one *immediately*." She pushed back, saying that for now, an app was an expensive "nice to have" that would require new hires and a lot of money to build. OK, I said, but to grow— and to make an investor like me believe she could be successful— she needed something to help her scale quickly. Fortunately for Rica, she had the customer base to bootstrap her business until she was good and ready to build her app—which she since launched in September 2017. "I'll say this," she said, when I asked her for an update, "having that app is what has allowed us to scale from three cities to sixty and add one hundred new professionals to our network a day."

Just to be clear: When I say *add tech*, I am not saying you have to custom-build an app like John and Rica did or even learn to code—in fact, that's not the right decision for many entrepreneurs. Most of your business needs are already served by an existing product that you could buy or license for a fraction of what it would cost to build. You've thought of something completely innovative and different? There's still probably a platform that's 70 percent of the way there that you could tweak to fit your needs. The folks at Breakout—which curates purpose-driven events for community leaders and startup founders—decided they needed an app to manage their annual gathering of 250 social entrepreneurs so that participants had a hub for communication in the lead-up to the event. The days before are a flurry of setting meetings, organizing shared accommodations, checking in, etc. It would have taken them months and good money to build their own platform, and it almost certainly wouldn't have been as good as the app they quickly decided to "white label," which is when you license an existing product but slap your logo on it so it looks like you made it. Furthermore, building it would have distracted them from their mission of supporting and inspiring social entrepreneurs.

There are so many great platforms out there just waiting to make your life easier. I know what it takes to build a tech product—and because of that, I tell people to *never* do it unless they absolutely have to. I sure wouldn't. In fact, when somebody on my team recently said, "Hey, Nathalie, we should build a BRAVA app for conversations and transactions with your portfolio companies and investors," I told her exactly that. "Love the idea. No effing way I'm going to build that. Go out and find me someone who already has."

I urge you to leapfrog with technology—but only after seriously considering your needs and expertise. You don't want to find you've spent good money and valuable time building something that you could have just bought or licensed, ready-to-go, from someone else!

Hack 14

Climb in Bed
with Your Customer

ENTREPRENEURS TEND TO lose sleep over their competitors. Misplaced anxiety! Stress out over your customers, and no one else.

I meet and evaluate startups every day. The most important thing I look for—what really makes me think they have a shot—is the degree to which they fixate on their customers. I want them not just to be obsessed but crazy obsessed. I want them to know what their client eats, drinks, thinks, worries about. I want to see that their customer is so important, and in such close communication, that they are playing a leading role in how the product or service develops. The companies that really *partner* with customers are the ones that are able to race past competitors, even when others may have had a head start.

I always go back to Tanya Menendez, whom I talked about in hack 8. Her company Maker's Row helps designers find and work with a factory to produce their goods at scale, which is often a real barrier to growth. Tanya was intimately familiar with this problem. Not long after graduating college, she founded a small leather goods line called the Brooklyn Bakery. Her biggest hurdle on the road to profitability was finding a factory. And in Brooklyn in

2011, she was surrounded by other creative, industrious makers with exactly the same problem. She convinced her partner at the Bakery, Matthew Burnett, to help her start a second company, a tech platform to help artisans find American factories to work with.

Tanya and Matthew had a head start on getting to know the customer. They *were* the customer. But they only knew about leather goods production—nothing about apparel, furniture, and packaging, all of which are now represented among the ten thousand factories and makers who list at Maker's Row.

"I really love to understand customers deeply and intimately. I want to understand everything about them," Tanya says. She went into overdrive. She went to factories and sat on the floor or in the head office for a twelve-hour day, getting to know everything about the owners and their problems. She learned what phones they used, what experiences triggered them, what they had to do to collect money. She even went to a factory owner's wedding. (Not to conduct research, but wow, what better way to learn about someone than a high-stress, multigenerational family celebration?)

"Everything that is the nuance that really makes a difference is so, so important to me," she says. "Sometimes the only way to learn is to actually be their peer and sit next to them and spend hours with them. . . . That's what really helped us have the customer insights to help us grow and market and sell."

To get to know factory owners even better, she started a dinner series. "We facilitated conversations around their own pain points and struggles. None of it was for the purpose of our own company gain; it was all for knowledge exchange," she says. She heard stories she never would have heard over emails or conference calls or through surveys. And of course, her team members benefited from this more candid, complete view of their everyday struggles. It allowed her and Matthew to shape Maker's Row into a custom-fit for their problems.

One mistake I see entrepreneurs make all the time is in thinking they own the solution. Your job is to own the problem—to say, I'm going to be as curious as I can and as smart as I can about meeting a need. Tanya saw that small designers had no idea how to find and interface with manufacturing partners while American factories were struggling to compete in a global marketplace. Her customers shaped the solution every step of the way. For example, one of Maker's Row's most popular features, email courses on sourcing and manufacturing, wasn't a part of Tanya's original vision. Neither was the site's Projects feature, which guides entrepreneurs through a process of providing the information factories need to make bids. She had learned that designers' challenges went way beyond finding factories; they had a knowledge gap, which made the task of signing on with a factory at all completely overwhelming.

It's never too early to embrace your market. Approach your customer early—as in, right away, the moment you see the problem. Ask them to develop the solution with you, and you're much more likely to get it right.

Worship the Franchise

DON'T TELL ME there's nothing sexy about a franchise. First of all, if you think it's all fast food and fluorescent lights, you're wrong. There are opportunities in everything from childcare to spas to automotive services.

Franchises are the ideal entry into entrepreneurship. Where some see paint-by-numbers constraint, I see a proven brand and system. Where some see corporate nonsense, I see an expert support team focused on your success. Where some see just a small business, I see a small business *plus* a free education and a platform for leapfrogging to more ambitious endeavors. I also know that there's plenty of room to be creative and resourceful within the guidelines—and that's one reason some franchisees do better than others.

In fact, I'm so pro-franchise that I believe every small business should think like one from the very beginning—particularly if they want to get bigger. Franchise or fail! I don't mean you have to actually franchise out your business. But you do need to create clear, replicable processes that fine-tune every part of the experience a customer has with your business and your product. That's how you make the experience consistent, but it's also how you constantly improve. These processes should be so clear to everyone who works for you that you could pull out tomorrow and just sit back and watch the money roll in.

So many small business owners resist this, for a variety of reasons. They're enthralled with the secret sauce they believe they bring and think some "magic" is lost by creating business processes. Or they're in reactive mode, never taking the time to organize and document. Or ego is involved. They may not realize it, but deep down they fear that if they can teach someone else (or a thousand somebodies) to do exactly what they do, they'll no longer be special—or necessary.

If you want to be cured of these false anxieties, read my second-favorite business book (after Twyla Tharp's *The Creative Habit*): *The E-Myth Revisited: Why Most Small Businesses Don't Work and What to Do About It* by Michael Gerber. It's about as old-school as it gets, but it's as relevant and useful as it was in 1995, the year of its publication. (The original edition, *The E-Myth*, was published in 1986!) Gerber may be a bearded, bookish guy with glasses, but he manages to make replicable process and other lessons of franchising sexy. He completely changed my attitude about how to make a business truly magical (and rainmaking). The answer is not creative chaos, I promise you.

As Gerber writes, "The simple truth about the greatest businesspeople I have known is that they have a genuine fascination for the truly astonishing impact little things done exactly right can have on the world. . . . This book is a guide for those who see the development of an extraordinary business as a never-ending inquiry, an ongoing investigation, an active engagement with a world of forces, within us and without, that continually amaze and confound the true seekers among us with awesome variety, unending surprises, and untold complexity."

Is it getting warm in here?!

Fan yourself off and let's get started. To think like a franchiser from day 1, Gerber says to preoccupy yourself with three activities:

1. **Innovation.** Constantly look for better ways to get things done. Most small business owners put too much attention on innovating the product and not enough on innovating the experience of buying it. Get that right, and "the entire process by which the business does business is a marketing tool, a mechanism for finding and keeping customers." Gerber didn't know it at the time, but he was giving the same kind of advice that has made Zappos one of the leading companies of the new economy. (If you ever meet Zappos CEO Tony Hsieh, ask him for me if he read *The E-Myth*, and if not, tell him he'd like it.) Zappos sells the same shoes everyone else does, but it helps "deliver happiness" to customers (riffing on Hsieh's memoir title) by making even the tiniest aspects of the buying experience delightful—two-way shipping, useful product videos, customer service people who will do anything to make their clientele happy. And in return, their customers talk, blog, and tweet about Zappos like they're the second coming.

2. **Quantification:** Some of the most important numbers you need to make a business successful aren't in the profit and loss statement. You can't know whether something is an innovation if you have no way to measure its impact. Treat any tweaks like science: Measure before, measure after, and have a control. Turn every aspect of your business into numbers: daily sales, customer service inquiries, customer visits, etc.

3. **Orchestration:** Eliminate discretion in how your business operates. If you know something works, why would you let anyone do it any other way? Once you've proven that something works, it becomes part of the operating manual. This does *not* mean that the operating manual doesn't change. Your business dies on the vine if you aren't constantly looking for opportunities to innovate, test new ideas, and compare them to the normal routine. But you can't improve without a baseline.

These three building blocks cover the basics and create more space for the good stuff—the magic, the creativity, the passion. There's very little magic in struggling on your own in a subsistence business. And in Gerber's Zen-like telling, as you grow your business, you grow yourself.

Squeeze Out
Every Drop of Value

THE FORMER CFO of McDonald's famously said, "We're not technically in the food business. We're in the real estate business." What he meant was that McDonald's made more money by buying real estate and leasing it to franchise owners than it did from hamburger sales.

You don't need to be a cynical meat-patty mogul to work this hack. Whatever your core business, you owe it to yourself and your customer to be relentlessly creative about looking up and down the value chain to see where you can add revenue, improve margins, and create as much innovation as you can for the business and for your customers.

So what's a value chain? It's the term Harvard economist Michael Porter came up with to describe how a business takes raw materials and adds value in each step on the way to becoming a finished product, which customers will then buy for more than the business's costs. Smart entrepreneurs look up and down the chain to see where they can save money, make money, or find something new that customers will appreciate.

Victoria Flores immediately comes to mind, maybe because her product is about as raw as you can get: human hair extensions.

At first, Victoria—born in El Paso, Texas, the daughter of immigrants—wasn't looking to build a business. She was already making a healthy living at Morgan Stanley on the prime brokerage business consulting team (despite the fact that she went to school to become a physical therapist).

But Victoria had something she really wanted to punch: the insane cost to maintain hair extensions. As someone with frizzy, wild hair, she considered extensions a must and was spending hundreds of dollars every time she hit a salon. If you've ever gotten extensions, you know her pain.

Here's how many stylists work the value chain: with a total lack of transparency about where the hair they sell comes from or what it costs, which allows them to charge hundreds or even thousands of dollars to supply and weave in extensions. They like to talk up their "secret source" in, say, Malaysia or Peru. "All of it's a lie," Victoria told me. Meanwhile, wholesalers generally require buyers to prove they have a cosmetology license. The cheaper alternative is to find a no-frills beauty supply shop, but it can be hard to know what to buy.

Victoria and a friend—"a white girl from Alabama who's been wearing hair since birth"—got to talking and said to each other: "There's *got* to be a better way." They set out to find their own source, with a plan to keep some for themselves and sell the rest to friends. Finding quality, reliable product turned out to be a lot harder than they expected. But they kept going, working with suppliers they found on Google and Alibaba, the popular China-based search engine. They'd finally think they found a good source, and then the next batch would be a rat's nest. Doing the hard work of sourcing—which eventually forced them to jump on a plane to China—was the first and most important part of the value chain to crack. "We're very up front that our hair comes from India and then it's sent to China to get processed and cleaned because our Indian sources don't have the capabilities for that," she says.

Working directly with vendors in China was ultimately what led to a high-quality, reliable source that they started selling to friends, at a price much, much lower than they could find anywhere else. Then they could either put the extensions in themselves, or walk into a salon and say to the stylist, "Look, here's my hair. Now what are you going to charge me to put it in?" Naturally, the price drops way down because the only cost to the stylist is his or her labor.

Three years went by. Victoria and her partner looked up and realized they had sold $1 million of hair. This was no side hustle; it was a serious business. From there, Lux Beauty Club was born. The website makes the company's primary value-add loud and clear: "No middlemen, no secret pricing, no cosmetology license required. FULL PRICE TRANSPARENCY is our mission." And unlike most companies, they've got hair for every ethnicity.

At every step, they looked for ways to make things better and easier for customers, borrowing ideas whenever they saw a great one. They noticed that many women were coming back almost monthly—and the price was low enough that they could afford to! They studied the success of companies like Dollar Shave Club, which regularly sends out replacement razor cartridges to a loyal member base, and shifted to a similar subscription model, mailing new extensions on a schedule convenient to each user. Like Zappos, they encouraged women to order several colors and return what didn't work, so they could get exactly what they needed from their very first order. They created tutorials to help make it easy to find the right hair, and they are halfway through building an augmented-reality app to virtually "try on" different colors, textures, and lengths.

Marketing directly to the customer is Lux Beauty Club's core business, but they're working every angle of potential revenue. Many extensions come in basic, crappy packaging, since they are mostly purchased wholesale, not retail. Lux Beauty Club has upped the game with beautiful packaging, which customers like *and* which has secondary value for salons. Stylists can buy and display the hair, which makes for an easy upsell when they've got someone in the chair. Also in the works: Partnerships with blow-dry bars to add extensions to their services.

All that resourcefulness is paying off big: Lux Beauty Club is projecting $14 million in revenue by year three. Victoria has also been totally fearless in using hack 9 and cashing in on her woman card. "Not only am I a woman, but I'm also Latinx and I didn't go to Harvard. We were like, 'We're really screwed now,'" she jokes. But these "disadvantages" created real opportunities. For example, winning the Home Shopping Network's American Dreams contest, geared toward fast-tracking Latinx inventors, led to a coveted opportunity to sell a product—a clip-in hair bun—on the show. It did so well that they've been invited back to sell other products.

When Victoria first decided to source her own hair extensions, she had no idea how complex the terrain would be. She certainly didn't see herself getting on a plane to China. But most businesses are that way—and it's often in that dizzying complexity that you find those hidden opportunities to squeeze new value.

Laser in on an Empty Shelf

EVEN THE SMALLEST bodega in New York carries five brands of shampoo. Any product category you can think of, from soap to toys, is glutted with options. It's easy to feel like you need to be Jessica Alba or have a multimillion-dollar marketing budget to get attention for a new brand, product, or service.

So here's the trick: If you want to break through, don't try to create the brightest label or the loudest advertising campaign. Instead, find an empty shelf—a distribution space that's not clogged with competitors. Even better, a space that puts your product in an interesting or novel context that creates the impulse for someone to try something new.

Back in the early 2000s, I had Cranium as a client in Seattle; we were helping them translate the game for sale in a bunch of different countries, as well as create digital versions. It had just become the most successful board game in the U.S., but you couldn't find it in Toys"R"Us or any big-box store. They had no mass distribution. Instead, they customized their strategy to their target market, which was essentially yuppies. Where could they place the game so that this audience would not see it just once but many times, creating multiple opportunities for a purchase?

You can probably guess where this is going. Yuppies + Seattle = Starbucks. Aside from being the only game on the shelf, Starbucks offered another advantage. When people go to get a coffee, it's typically "me" time. They're indulging themselves, maybe feeling a little more playful or relaxed. And they need something to do while standing in line. (Seventeen years ago, most people weren't laser focused on the tech in their palms yet.)

To be clear, the founders were rich, white ex-Microsoft dudes with business cards that gave their titles as "Chief Noodler" and "The Grand Poobah," who managed to network their way into Charles Schulz's office. (The job titles were cute, but, women and people of color, I'm sorry to say, I wouldn't try that one at home. *Cute* is still the territory of those with strong social capital and a hell of a lot of privilege.) Fortunately, you don't have to have an in at a multinational corporation to work this hack. Any business at any size can find an empty shelf. I always say, "Find a way to be the yoga teacher at the electronics conference." If you go to a yoga conference, you're one of five thousand people all doing variations of the same thing. If you're a yoga teacher and you go to CES, where it's nothing but electronic geeks, you're an exotic animal. You're super cool or, at the very least, interesting. To use Seth Godin's visual, find a place where you're a purple cow.

Think expansively about two things: First, what's your customer's happy place? And second, what context will have them in buying mode? Amanda Hearst, the cofounder with Hassan Pierre of ethical fashion retailer Maison-de-Mode.com, quite possibly owes her business to this hack. She and Hassan got started in 2012 with a vision to show the luxury market that eco-fashion wasn't all Birkenstocks and rope shoes—it was chic and distinctive and had a story to tell. Hassan was a designer with his own line, and he knew a handful of other eco-fashion brands that were struggling for traction. Rather than knock on doors at Barneys or Saks and deal with old-school gatekeepers, Amanda and Hassan looked for informal, fun spaces where they could meet their customer directly. Their solution was concept pop-up stores, which weren't yet a "thing."

Their first pop-up was at Art Basel, a glitzy art fair that draws an international crowd. The choice was intentional. While Art Basel is flush with wealthy fashionistas, it's not a fashion event, "so we wouldn't get lost in the crowd," says Amanda. With merchandise from six brands on consignment, they took a cut on everything they sold and returned the rest to the designers.

The event was successful enough to pay for itself and for the next one—and so it went for five years. Pop-up after pop-up, each building their reputation and their customer base. Soon, people started reaching out to *them*. One of those calls led them to the Rosewood hotel in Georgetown, one of DC's toniest neighborhoods, setting up shop in a penthouse the weekend of the White House Correspondents' Association Dinner. Where better to make a mark than the total fashion desert that is bureaucratic DC? (Hey, Washingtonians, don't mind me; I'm a snotty New Yorker.) "That was one of our best shops, because people there were so happy to have cool clothing and a shopping experience," says Amanda. "Everyone was so excited."

Amanda didn't just find an empty shelf; she built her own. Now instead of selling six brands, they have more than seventy, all available through their website. They still don't have a warehouse, keeping overhead low. Instead, the brands maintain their own inventory and ship it out with Maison-de-Mode.com packaging. The pop-up strategy also allowed the company to leapfrog while their competitors (most of whom have gone bust) burned through startup capital. It wasn't until early 2017 that Maison-de-Mode.com accepted a round of funding and expanded its staff beyond the two founders and an intern. Amanda says operating lean will always be a top priority.

Whatever your business, I guarantee you there's a big empty

shelf that your customer is just waiting to be filled. It can be as small or as big as you're ready for. It is actually less about creativity and more about paying attention. If you draw a blank, get out there and follow your customers' lead. (Head back to hack 14, Climb in Bed with Your Customer.)

Hack 18

Passive Income Is Sweaty Work

Wouldn't it be great to have a revenue stream that you could set in motion and then let sit, just watching the money roll in? Of course it would be, which is why self-proclaimed financial gurus love to pitch their schemes on how to create so-called passive income. Write an ebook or two, create an online training course, then jet off to Thailand while your bank accounts grow five figures a month.

I call bullshit. Passive income is a myth. My girl Jovanka Ciares, whose mission is to help women recover from autoimmune illnesses, has been working her butt off for six years to build and sell her online programs and ebooks (aka *infoproducts*) and has been in the business of health for fifteen. She is the opposite of passive. Jovanka says, "There is no such thing as *do nothing, make money*. Unless you are Donald Trump, or somebody who inherited a lot of money, or you were one of the first investors in cigarettes." There's no product out there, physical or virtual, that doesn't require maintenance. Everything from ATMs to infoproducts sometimes break down. Long-term investing is as passive as it gets, but to Jovanka's point, you need to throw a huge amount of money into the market and assume some risk if you want to live off your earnings.

That doesn't mean what's traditionally called *passive income* can't be a useful tool. But let's be real and call it *less-active income*. Let's also acknowledge it can require an Olympic sprint—not to mention real financial investment—to get started. Jovanka will set you straight about what it really requires. "By the time you see somebody's story of success splattered all over social media, there's been years, literally years of hustle," she says. Best-case scenario, it can be a way to add a revenue stream by drawing in customers who might spend money on your other products if they're satisfied with the first one. For example, a small deli with an ATM may bring in customers who need cash but who also decide to buy a soda or sandwich.

In some ways, Jovanka is about as well positioned as anyone could be. She's got evergreen content, the kind that will still be fresh and in-demand five years from now. She was on an ABC TV show called *My Diet Is Better Than Yours*, which led to press hits like *ET* and *People*. She's got a user-friendly website with updated content and resources that will appeal to her long-standing fans and new readers alike. She's a great face for her brand—gorgeous and full of warmth and passion to help people. But she also has real challenges, because she's competing in the very crowded health and wellness space.

When Jovanka set out to launch her first product five years ago, a four-week guided online detox program, she started from almost nothing. She had a coaching business but no email list and only a small community of social media followers. For six months, she spent about twenty hours a week developing the product and building the infrastructure. She hired a consultant to help put all the pieces together, particularly the tech. She found a joint venture partner who sold the detox program to her email list in exchange for 50 percent of the revenue. All in all, she spent about $5,000. All in all, she made about $5,000.

Financially, it was a wash, but she left with an expanded list, enhanced brand recognition, and the knowledge to do it again—faster, better, and without a coach. Several dozen of her most enthusiastic followers pay thirty-five dollars a month to be part of her online community, where she teaches two hours a month. Her ebooks are now part of that offering, so that's huge value for her clients, and she hired someone part-time to take care of technical maintenance. But the only "passive" income she's earning is about $250 a month from the people who Google their way to buying her ebooks.

The good news is that while Jovanka's always hustling, she's largely killing two birds with one stone. She spends most of her product-related time doing the stuff that lights her up—teaching and interacting with members on their journey to health—and more important, the marketing work she does pushes juice into every aspect of her business. Anything she does on social media feeds her online community, as well as her coaching and speaking business, which is currently the biggest contributor to her livelihood.

The online community is where Jovanka feels she's really serving her mission, because unlike one-on-one coaching, it's affordable for almost everybody. "Based on my projections, it'll take me about eighteen to twenty-four months to get to a point where I have enough members in the community that I can consider it my main source of income, and I can drop everything else that I'm doing and focus all my energy there," she says.

Jovanka is also constantly on the lookout for partners who can help promote her products to their email lists and communities. She just struck a deal with a personal organizer to offer a health webinar to her subscribers and social networks. She will be selling to her community, but who knows what else will come out of it?

In a perfect world, your new less-active income stream won't add costs to your business. For example, you don't hire someone to fix your ATMs; you train an existing employee to handle it. If you can create similar efficiencies in your own business, less-active income can be a great tool to give your balance sheet a boost.

Hack 19

When the Bar's Low, Dance on It

WHEN YOU'RE RUBBING two pennies together, you can feel the urge to scrimp or to sacrifice your own values for industry norms. Resist it. Figure out what values differentiate your product, and stick to them relentlessly.

Jerry Murrell, the founder of Five Guys, was a father of four when he and his wife opened their first store. I'm a vegetarian, so I'm not a customer, but I was taken by his story on Guy Raz's NPR podcast *I Built This*. He and his family decided that unlike most burger joints, they weren't going to compete on price or convenience. They were going to compete on quality. When it came to where to source his French fries, he didn't screw around. He went out back behind the most popular French fry hut on the boardwalk in Ocean City, Maryland, found the boxes the potatoes came in, and wrote down the name of the farm. Soon he was their best customer.

He put his kids, barely out of high school and uninterested in college, in charge of sourcing things like mayonnaise, ketchup, pickles, and the other toppings the brand is now known for. He never let them see the prices and told them to just pick what tasted best. When the numbers got out of balance, they didn't hunt for cheaper ingredients. They raised the price of the burger. They're now an international franchise with more than $1 billion in annual revenue, and they're among the leaders of the trend toward higher-quality fast food. Traditional burger joints like McDonald's have had to completely reinvent themselves in the effort to be just a little bit more like Five Guys.

Being proud of your product will make you more successful, and it also increases the chance that you'll create a real legacy. In 2014, Carrie Hammer was approaching a major milestone as a designer: her very first New York Fashion Week show as part of an emerging designer showcase. She and her stylist, Engie Hassan, were clicking through their checklist—lighting, DJ, makeup aesthetic—and when they got down to models, Carrie realized she had a problem. Carrie's mission is to give kick-ass businesswomen of all shapes and sizes dresses that they'll look and feel great in. She knew that the models the agencies would send were unlikely to resemble her customers. In fact, they were likely to represent ideals of beauty that she was pushing against.

The fastest, most efficient way to move forward would have been to go with the flow and use the resources being handed to her. But it didn't sit right. "My clients at the end of the day are CEOs of companies; they are moguls; and they are women, not models who often start as young as twelve, models I've sometimes even seen do their algebra homework backstage," she says. Pressured to make a choice, she had an epiphany: "My clients are role models; they're not runway models." She created and trademarked the Role Models Not Runway Models campaign, and a movement was born. When her collection debuted, the women rocking her couture were not models but actual customers.

It was not easy. Working with role models instead of fashion models meant custom-fitting the dresses to every size and shape. It meant helping founders and CEOs overcome their nerves and strut proudly down the catwalk. (I know—I was one of them!) But when it was all over, she had made waves across the world as both the fashion and mainstream press went wild. She was invited back to the next four New York Fashion Weeks and even to one in Shanghai. More than 120 companies have followed suit, expanding their beauty standards even in the rarefied world of high fashion. Over the next three years, Carrie received more than a billion global media impressions and was a number one trending brand on Facebook and Twitter. She garnered global recognition and acclaim for the #RoleModelsNotRunwayModels movement and the Role Models Not Runway Models™ campaign.

At Carrie's third New York Fashion Week, she lost a financial sponsor at the last minute and thought she was going to have to pull out. But when the women walking in her show heard the news, they all stepped up and bought dresses—because they loved them *and* because they believed in Carrie's vision. She ended up with more funds than she was expecting from the lost sponsor. Every entrepreneur will have her ups and downs. Keep your integrity and ideals close, and you'll find that climbing out of the troughs is a lot easier—particularly because you'll have many friendly hands waiting to pull you up.

SECTION 3

Go

Building a tribe—a powerful network of people who'll make a clutch call on your behalf as readily as they'll back you in a bar fight—will slam the accelerator on your business. With every ally you create, you move forward faster. Getting things done becomes increasingly easier and infinitely more fun.

When it comes to broadening your circle, intentionality is the leapfrogger's best friend. It's the clever shortcut to overcoming limitations when you lack proximity and pedigree. Have you ever wondered why New York and other big cities are full of lonely, disconnected people? They have access to every resource imaginable, but few really take advantage. That's your secret weapon.

So if you're stuck in a one–Dairy Queen town or didn't go to Harvard, don't worry about it. Do the work. Expand your network by reaching out, paying attention, creating value, and learning the rules of every ecosystem you encounter—and in some cases, redefining them to create the spaces you, and others like you, need.

Hack 20

Find Your Dolores Huerta

WHEN I SAW Gloria Steinem onstage with Dolores Huerta before an Athena Film Festival screening of the documentary *Dolores*, Gloria said something about Dolores that really moved me, about her early days of activism with the history-altering labor and civil rights leader. When Dolores called, she'd ask Gloria to do things Gloria had no idea how to do. But since Dolores seemed so confident she was up to these tasks, she dug in and figured them out. "Without you," said Gloria to Dolores, "I would never have known what I was capable of."

I loved hearing this from a woman I admire so much, because it reminded me of many of the relationships I've sought out with wise women. They come to me from a place of accomplishment, and assume I can meet them there. I'm able to grow faster by trying to see myself the way they see me and grow into that.

I want you to Pinterest your network. In the same way that people "pin" their dream backyard, couch, or wedding dress, I want you to be relentlessly aspirational as you build your circle of contacts. Don't just think one step beyond your existing circle, even if you've already "hacked" it with a mastermind (hack 6). Set your sights on people who you don't think you'd ever organically connect with, people doing amazing things in your industry or area of interest. Today these people are your aspirations; tomorrow they're your colleagues and collaborators. You need the Dolores Huerta to your Gloria Steinem. People who can stand on their mountain and describe opportunities that you can't yet see. You also need this kind of network to connect you to the practical resources that make these expanded dreams possible: lawyers, financiers, CEOs. Experts at going big.

My Dolores is Kathryn "Kitty" Kolbert. She is the lawyer who argued the 1992 landmark Supreme Court case *Planned Parenthood v. Casey*, which is credited with saving *Roe v. Wade*. More recently, she stepped in as the director of Barnard's Athena Center for Leadership Studies. When she asked me to advise her, I was more than a little intimidated. What skill or resource could I have that would help a woman whose passion, practice, and wit had given millions of women control over their reproductive futures and saved countless women's lives in the decades since the historic decision? What power did she see in me that I hadn't yet understood myself? Kitty gave me the confidence to step into advocacy with an ambition I had previously only funneled into tech. If I had not met her, my life would look very different. I might not be writing this book.

So sit down, fire up the internet, and start building a list: Who out there can push you to unlock your own power? Who is making waves in your space internationally, nationally, and regionally? Then think local: Who is doing interesting things in your own city or town? The moment this circle of people becomes concrete, it becomes achievable.

Building this list is itself an important education. You'll learn more about the shape of your industry. You'll see new possibilities for where to take your business, and in reading about these people, you may even pick up tactics you can put to use right now. This is also the moment to find IRL networking opportunities. If you're in a big city, you'll have to weed through hundreds of live events—so again, be intentional about who you want to meet: their work, their values, their lifestyles. Use that as your filter. If you're in a small town, you may not have that many options for in-person networking—but don't assume you can't create one. Try starting your own Meetup group, for example. If you can't raise a crowd locally, what if you instead think about places you could day-trip to, say, the radius within a two-hour drive? Once you expand your horizon, the picture may start to look a lot better. Universities, community colleges, chambers of commerce, the Small Business Administration, nearby conferences, and non-profits are all ideal places to start.

Leapfroggers need aspirational networks—and eventually real-life mentors—more than anyone. In 2017, at the high school summer startup boot camp I created at Barnard, I told the thirty young women who had bravely flown in from all over the world that my Catholic, family-oriented parents weren't exactly sup-portive when I decided to leave home for college. They worried about me, and they worried I was abandoning them.

Afterward, a girl from a town in rural Texas came up to me and started crying. "My family thinks I'm conceited and that I think I'm better than them because I want to leave Texas," she said. I gave her a big hug, and we talked some more. That day I left campus feeling as though just hearing my story—and learning how well things had worked out, not just with my career but with my family, too—had helped lift some of the weight off her shoulders.

So many people struggle both emotionally and practically with the burden of their family's or community's disapproval. Immi-grants who fear losing the values of the old country. Religious families who worry their children will lose god. Close-knit racial or economic communities that see upward mobility as a form of assimilation, aka "selling out." Having a dream that your family or community doesn't share can be crushing. I'm sure it keeps many would-be business leaders from taking the first step and others from expanding beyond a certain limited view of what's possible or acceptable. A local restaurant? *OK*. A local restaurant your parents couldn't afford to eat at? *Sellout*. A restaurant app that will require you to move to Silicon Valley? *Pipe dream!*

When you step outside of boundaries circumscribed by the people around you, you need role models. You need to be able to see and taste what success on your terms looks like and learn how to approach challenges with knowledge that lies outside your own cultural and economic status quo. You won't ever forget who you are, but you need freedom to leave the nest, make it big, and come back to do right by the very same people who doubted you. Often that means building a new community to support you. You can live in two worlds, and the best way to show your community you didn't sell out is to do just that: Show them.

When I hugged that crying camper, I told her what it felt like to take my mom to the inauguration of Mayor Eric Garcetti as a VIP. She has lived in Los Angeles for more than forty years but had never met a sitting mayor. And two weeks later, my mom was again with me at a proud moment when we launched Galvanize in Chicago for the United State of Women. She got to hang out with legends like Valerie Jarrett and Tina Tchen, so you can say she's come around. There's still plenty of stuff I do that makes my mother mouthy, but she knows—and I try to constantly remind her through my actions—that no matter how I grow, my family and the important values they passed on to me travel with me everywhere.

Hack 21

Silicon Valley, Bye

B E A BIG fish in a small pond. Why launch in a major metropolis where costs and competition are both skyscraper-high? Consider moving to a smaller hub or even to your hometown, where you have family and community resources.

Tech entrepreneurs: You don't need no stinkin' Silicon Valley. There was a day when investors wouldn't even talk to you if you weren't based in the Valley or another major hub. Not anymore. You just need to know how to work the upside.

Sheena Allen is a badass founder I met when we both spoke at a Tech808 conference in Washington, DC. She started an app development firm when she was still at the University of Southern Mississippi. She wasn't a techie, but she saw a need and decided to do something about it. She drew the design for that first app, a tool to store and track receipts, on a piece of computer paper. Then she borrowed $3,500 from her father—a huge sum for him, and she has since paid back every penny—and hired a foreign developer to build it. The app flopped. The next one did a little better, still a far cry from a home run. But the third, a camera app called Dubblen that cost her $2,500, scored five hundred thousand downloads in three months and kept on climbing. This was the moment, she thought, to go big—move to Silicon Valley, find a mentor, and get investment. Once there, though, she hit a wall. Investors told her the business wasn't ready for venture funding.

After a stint in Austin, Texas, her apps now had a million total downloads, but she still hadn't found funding for the business. So Sheena returned to Mississippi, frustrated and looking for a new problem to punch, one with more growth potential than photo and video apps, a tougher nut to crack now that the market was so crowded. Before long, she was focused on a major problem she saw everywhere in Jackson, her Mississippi hometown: the unbanked.

Sheena's new financial technology (fintech) startup, CapWay, is headquartered in New York, and there's a good reason why: "You get a better valuation if you're a New York company, in fintech. The zip code makes you sound like you're better than you are." But Sheena spends most of her time in Mississippi, the heart of CapWay's test launch. She's raised funds from two individual angel investors, along with three investment institutions: Liberty Bank, the second-largest African American owned bank; Power-Moves USA, a national initiative to support high-growth minority entrepreneurs; and Backstage Capital, Arlan Hamilton's investment firm, mentioned earlier.

With that disappointing trip to the Valley and six years of progress under her belt, Sheena can now see the upside to incubating a business and developing chops outside of the major hubs. Here are four examples:

1. **You're closer to the problem.** CapWay is focused on an underserved market—the unbanked and underbanked, people who are working poor. "The large region with those residents is in the South. It's not in New York; it's not in Silicon Valley," says Sheena. "In fact, I talk to investors in Silicon Valley or New York who really have no clue what I'm talking about when I tell them that people keep money in their mattresses.

That's not what they know. I can talk to my staff in Mississippi, or even in Florida, Alabama, or Arkansas, they're going to know exactly what I'm talking about. I personally feel that a lot of the inner circle of the tech world in Silicon Valley, even in LA, New York, those major tech hubs, they don't understand these real-world problems. But they do understand that there's a lot of money to make from them. Financial inclusion is a $400 billion industry. But I think it actually takes people from outside of those major tech hubs, to truly make it work."

2. **It's easier to run lean and leapfrog.** "We have an office in Mississippi, and it's $50 per person in a shared space. A full office will still only cost like $450 a month. You pay $450 for a shared desk even in a small hub," she says. Because there was no local tech industry when she started out, Sheena's always worked with overseas developers she hires through guru.com or upwork.com. "Some people I know had a bad experience working with overseas developers. But I'll tell you, if you're bootstrapping it, you're just trying to make it, you deal with it. You work out the kinks and jump over the hurdles," she says.

3. **The networking is better.** "It's not like you have to go through ten different degrees to try to get to *the one*. If you're in a small hub, you probably make a phone call or send an email; somebody's gonna know somebody," says Sheena. She secured her two most helpful mentors to date through a cold email and a LinkedIn request. She also became close to a local business professor, whom she met at Jackson's Tech Meetup. He made many phone calls and introductions on her behalf. Sheena says that small-town opportunity in tech has grown: "The fact is that every area, regardless of how small or how big it is, in one way or another, is building tech infrastructure. I think that's a gift that you have now that I didn't necessarily have in 2012."

4. **Investors are starting to see the upside.** "A lot of smaller hubs are now coming up with their own investment models. Two years ago, that wasn't possible. You had to really go to the Valley or New York to get money. Don't get me wrong, they still have a long way to go, but I look at how far Atlanta has come in the last five years. I look at where Miami is, New Orleans, Cincinnati. Oh my gosh, who thought, *I want to move to Cincinnati for tech,* five years ago? Nobody. There are numerous investment teams now that invest only in companies in the South," she says. Even investors in the Valley and New York City are broadening their horizons. In her early days, Sheena was told by many investors that she'd need to be operating in a larger city to be considered. "A lot of those same investors or those same firms have now done away with that. They don't care where you are, as long as you can come out there for those meetings, for those follow-ups. I think even the major tech investors realize that it can be done from anywhere now," she says.

Don't Wait for Folks
to Get Woke

Recently I spent an afternoon falling in love with a bustling, high-energy accelerator in Newark, New Jersey, called Fownders, started by my fellow Latinx entrepreneur Gerard Adams. The peak came when we walked over to the cafeteria and they were serving arepas. I nearly choked up. *Arepas.* Arepas mean family to me.

At a time when every inch of progress seems to be taking two steps backward, there was something incredibly inspiring about seeing arepas and tech founders under one roof. Brown tech, in the flesh. Here was a little pocket of hope.

Did the 2016 presidential election finally make it clear that we're not past any isms or phobias? These strange times, during which so much progressive change seems to be rolling back, can be dark and often draining. I know I'm not alone in sometimes needing a haven—a place where all I see, hear, and feel is optimism and power. A place that feels like home.

Half of my inspiration for this book was to bring to the surface the million cool ways people are creating their own light. But it wasn't until I was talking to Trabian Shorters, the founder of the BMe Community, a national network of community builders, that I realized that there was not just an important hack here but an entire history behind the organizations, aka pockets of hope, that were created for safety, security, and, in fact, for leapfrogging, by racial and ethnic groups and by people who shared a common trade.

A history lesson: The first female bank president in the U.S. was a black woman named Maggie Lena Walker. She became president of the St. Luke Penny Savings Bank in 1902, in Richmond, Virginia, of all places, just a few decades since it was a slave state. She didn't become president by finding the woke-est white bank of the turn-of-the-century. Such a thing barely exists today; it certainly didn't exist then. No, she became president by starting her *own* bank through the Independent Order of St. Luke, the organization at which she had been rising in the leadership ranks since she was fourteen.

St. Luke was what was called a *mutual benefit society*. There were lots of them at the time, founded to provide services such as life insurance that black citizens and many other ethnic groups were shut out of. These orders filled practical needs like financial security when dealing with birth, death, and illness, but they did much more. Their dynamic was fraternalism, not charity. They preached self-reliance, community pride, preservation of cultural rituals, and, above all, working together to build the institutions that would improve the members' quality of life at a time when the rest of the country treated them as invisible.

Trabian Shorters carried the mutual benefit society model into the present with BMe Community, focused on black men. The idea is this: Most mass communication about black men these days, not unlike in Maggie Lena Walker's day, reads like a smear campaign. If a black man is in the news, he's either a criminal or a professional athlete (who, incidentally, are one kneel away from being talked about like criminals). Even the "good guys" contribute to this negative messaging: Social justice organizations designed to help black men often bring focus to the worst statistics in order to raise funding for their inarguably important work.

Inspired by organizations like the one that made Ms. Walker a bank president, Trabian decided he would hack this sick culture and lift up black men by creating a community where their contributions to society, not their community's challenges, were the locus of conversation. This was 2013, before #blacklivesmatter was a national rallying cry. Lots of people told him to back away slowly from the idea of forming a race-based group. "Knowledgeable people warned me that it would be a disaster," Trabian told BlackEnterprise.com. "Race is the third rail. 'It's a career-ender,' I was warned. They were well-meaning but mistaken." Since the nonprofit launched, membership has grown wildly. BMe leaders—aka "Community Geniuses"—are driving projects all over the country to lift up one another, better their communities, and build institutions to help one another thrive. Trabian and Ben Jealous, the former president and CEO of the NAACP, edited a book called *Reach: 40 Black Men on Living, Leading, and Succeeding*, which became a *New York Times* bestseller. Clearly BMe Community is serving a widely felt need. There are literally *dozens* of such groups for women as well—but it will take some research to discover which are active and influential in your town.

As clear as I am that there's no such thing as a post-racial America, I do understand the people who initially warned off Trabian. There was a time when I feared that publicly affiliating myself with women's networking or business support groups would make me look weak. I always mentored and championed talented women—but covertly, in back channels. I didn't want to divert my attention or be known to colleagues as the "rah-rah sisterhood" type. I wasn't running a charity; I was trying to get things done. That was my brand and my mission, and mentoring or advising other women was something I did in my private time. Since then I've come to the conclusion that being covert about helping other women wasn't serving anyone. Many women out there were no doubt holding back as well, and as a result, too many of us were working in silos, limiting our ability to help others and, in the worst case, suffering alone. There's only one thing worse than looking weak, I came to realize, and that's *being* weak. If you operate alone, it can happen more easily than you might like to think.

Joining a mutual benefit society, or simply creating informal spaces that function in a similar spirit, isn't about isolating yourself within your gender, race, etc. We are all in many communities, serving many purposes. In the words of the great patriot poet (and closeted gay man) Walt Whitman, "I am large, I contain multitudes." To own that a race-, culture-, or gender-based space might be beneficial to you doesn't mean closing yourself off to other opportunities or to the possibility that your big break or best friend might be someone who has never eaten, let alone made, an arepa. (Replace *arepa* with your own family favorite.)

Loads of women I know are already members of mutual benefit societies, many of them with Facebook outposts that create a space where even nonmembers can benefit. Dreamers // Doers is one of the best. Marquina Iliev-Piselli, a New York–based publishing entrepreneur, has been a member since 2016. She describes it this way: "Honestly, when I started I thought it was going to be 'fluffy' or not worth my time or the $50 monthly fee—but it's been totally worth it. Beyond the networking and accountability, it's a weekly emailed list of legitimate opportunities that help you personally and professionally grow." You have to find a member to sponsor your application, but you can join the free, closed Facebook group—where members share jobs and gigs—by answering a couple of easy questions.

We all need an inspiring space where real-life happy endings are happening to people who look and feel like us; where we know others' expectations will push our bar higher instead of bring us down. Trabian says, "Don't define yourself or people as the chump, the vic, or the minority character in someone else's story. As my son Malcolm would say, 'Know your worth.' This lets you add new chapters to the stories of your relentlessness. The story you tell yourself will create the life that you live."[1]

I've seen it again and again: The only thing more powerful in getting things done than self-interest is mutual interest. So get out there, find your people, and make a community that works for—and with—you.

Hack 23

Learn the Rules of
the New Clubhouse

OLD-FASHIONED NETWORKING—A BUNCH of professionals in a ballroom trading chitchat and business cards—is dead. I was at an event at the UN recently, surrounded by Millennials, when some poor schmuck asked a dirty question: "So, where do you *network*?" Everyone visibly cringed. Young professionals today—and increasingly, the rest of us—do not network. We *connect*.

So how are the most cutting-edge entrepreneurs hacking this tired notion? They're joining the cool-kids clubs such as Breakout, Young Global Leaders, Summit, TED, and Sundance. These organizations are in the business of creating meaningful experiences that inspire connection. Their members snowboard together. Glamp together. Sail together. Dance together. It's unorthodox if you're used to the old-school conference model, but this is increasingly how business relationships are made. And while this shift in style, focus, and tone may have been led by techies and Millennials, it's going mainstream. In fact, half of BRAVA's advisors come from the powerful network of young philanthropists and impact investors that my dear friend Rachel Cohen Gerrol founded, called Nexus.

This brave new world may look wild and free, but it has its own unspoken codes of conduct. I have seen many newcomers crash and burn, hard, because they don't understand how these new—and, let's be clear, elite—communities operate. Here are your crib notes to fitting in.

Impact is the new status symbol. The organizations I've mentioned are exclusive by design. Their events are generally invite-only and expensive, to the tune of thousands of dollars. But here's the good news: Access to and status within these communities is within your reach. A Tesla never hurts, but the most highly rated currency here isn't in your wallet; it's in your actions—your *impact*. How much good are you doing in the world? Is your work exciting? More important, is it meaningful—or can you convince me it is?

Identify the ways in which your work is meaningful, and perfect your elevator pitch for articulating that to others. Maybe you have a business with baked-in social impact, like Thinx period underwear. Every time a customer buys a pair, Thinx sends money to the AFRIpads organization in Uganda, where girls routinely miss school while menstruating because they can't afford pads, to fund seven washable pads.

But social entrepreneurship isn't a requirement. Steve Jobs said that things don't have to change the world to be important. Seeing that your work is personally meaningful to *you* can be incredibly inspiring to the people you meet. For example, say a guy tells me he has a weight-loss app. On the face of it, I'm unimpressed: *Another tool to pressure women to obsess about weight. Thanks, guy.* But say this person tells me he's passionate about ending the obesity epidemic. Honestly, I'm probably still not sold, but my authenticity meter is set to maximum sensitive. But say he then tells me he lost his grandmother and mother to obesity-related illnesses and was teased mercilessly in grade school because he was chunky. Then I start to care. He's told me what's near and dear to his heart. I feel him.

Each of us has some honest, deeply felt reason why our work and our goals are meaningful. And hopefully, directly or indirectly, we're all on a mission to do some good. Find it, shape it, share it.

Don't ask to be on the list. The kiss of death is to email one of these orgs and say, "Can you please invite me to your event?" (I have met one woman who did that successfully, once—but the event in question was starving for women.) Generally speaking, that's not the way to endear yourself to an essentially elitist crew. The best way in is to do something so incredible that the organizers hear about it and seek you out. I know, easier said than done. If you're not there yet, next best is to connect with two or three people within the community or event you want to access and get them to recommend you. (See hack 20, Find Your Dolores Huerta.) One person vouching for you is a fluke. Three people says, "Wow, this person is really hot right now. Let's bring them in."

I won't lie: Sometimes, even if you get invited, the admission price is still going to be the door slamming in your face. But there are always people who don't pay face value. They've either done something notable that gets them invited as a speaker, or they find something to trade. An acquaintance of mine had a nonprofit that wasn't particularly well-known, but that connected her to powerful women politicians. So she earned her keep by assembling a panel of heavy hitters. Maybe you have a huge mailing list or access to the press. Figure out what's important to the organization, and if you can, offer up a barter. Otherwise, save, save, save, and make it your annual vacation.

Never solicit. A few years ago I was at an event at Sundance, surrounded by wealthy "big deal" types. But in the moment, none of that mattered. It was late, and we were all sitting by a fireplace, chilling, talking about movies and getting to know one another. Everyone there was hip to the new networking—except for one woman, a wonderful struggling filmmaker, who didn't get it. When one of the heavy hitters expressed casual interest in her work, she shifted immediately to formal pitch mode. "Would you like to step outside and hear about my next project?" she asked him.

Man, did she kill the vibe. She killed it hard. Everyone just stared at her. It ruined the moment for that poor guy, who suddenly felt more like a wallet than a human being. And it ruined it for everyone else, too. I felt really sorry for her. "Ah, man. She doesn't get it," I thought. That's not how we hang. If she had gotten to know the guy and had a little patience, who knows what might have happened someday.

You've got to throw out the old "hurry up and pitch" and "always be closing" mind-sets. It's like trying to build a semi-conductor with hammer and nails.

Here's how I met my current business partner: We were at a ski weekend for about one hundred entrepreneurs, hosted by one of the more infamous cool-kids clubs, which claims to be social impact–oriented. We both arrived a little skeptical, a little sourpuss. Ironically, that was our first point of connection. We became immediate friends. (Another hack: If you can't honestly smile, find the other person who's frowning.) We started talking about the inherent problem of diversity in exclusive networks and about how women get shut out. It turned out that he was an investor who wanted to work more actively to make the world a better place for his two daughters and women in general. We connected over that shared passion and kept the conversation up after going back to our respective homes. But it wasn't until months later that he called me up and said, "I'm going to build a new firm focused on impact. Let's find a way to work together."

Opportunities, not asks. So you're focused on building relationships. That doesn't mean that there's no acceptable "ask." I will never say to someone, "Here's what I'm doing; will you invest?" I'll say, "I'm super passionate about this. If you know anyone who you think is similarly passionate and can help, will you introduce me?" I'm not pressuring them to do anything other than invite someone into a club that they'll think is cool. It's not an ask at all—it's an opportunity. Sometimes the person even surprises me by saying, "Actually, I might be the investor you're looking for."

I'm a direct person. There are times when this roundabout approach feels silly. But the truth is, when you're meeting new people—in this connection-oriented context, but really in most contexts—it's absolutely necessary. It's how trust is built.

There's an old-school sales tactic that tells you to get a potential client to say yes seven times in a negotiation. It's behavioral psychology: You're actually training their brain to say "yes." Call me cynical, but "connecting" isn't so different. As you strike up a conversation with a new friend, you're looking for the common ground that has you saying "yes, yes, yes" to each other. Once you've done that, everything about you becomes a potential "yes"—even if you come to a point in the conversation when normally they might have said no. They keep the momentum going. You've opened their mind—and *that's* the new art of connecting.

Hack 24

The Four-Word Phrase
That Gets Shit Done

Y OU'RE LAUNCHING A business, or you're in the early stages.
You've got a thousand items on your to-do list and a clock
ticking. Here's my personal shortcut to plowing through every
to-do list I've ever written: Throw it out. Spend some time working on other people's lists instead. Weirdly enough, this approach
helps me beat the clock on my own problems again and again. The
four-word phrase that gets the most done isn't *What do I need?* It's
What do you need?

I'm known as a person who can solve seemingly complex problems in five minutes by sending out a group text. There's a simple
reason I have the network I have and why they do what they can
when I ask.

Taylor Barnes, who launched the United State of Women in
partnership with the Obama White House, clued me in to the
reason. She's a busy woman, and everyone from politicians to
brand reps was constantly scrambling for access to her platform.
But one day she told me, "Nathalie, no matter what I'm doing,
you're one person whose call I always take, the person who I'll
always try to help—because you are the only person whose first
words are always, *What do you need?*"

I go through life trying to offer six times as much as I ask for, and it has apparently earned me a reputation for giving more than I take. In the year before we launched BRAVA Investments, I went even further, hitting my network with a generosity bomb. I probably shifted my ratio to about 100:1—in other words, I was not just saying yes to every request for my help, I was actively reaching out and asking how I could help people in my network. I knew that when my company launched, I'd be leaning on others for a while.

So I challenge you to put away your to-do list every so often. Maybe it's once a week or once a month. Spend a day devoting yourself to connecting with people in your network and looking for ways to be useful. Make a habit of being both reflexively and systematically generous. By reflexively, I mean taking the opportunities that come your way, whether it's answering someone's social media request for a restaurant rec, attending an out-of-the-way birthday party, making an introduction, or spending twenty minutes critiquing someone's work.

By systematically, I mean exactly that: a system. Schedule time or develop a ritual that works for you. In the same way some people tithe their income 10 percent, you can tithe your calendar 10 percent. That's half a day a week spent helping people you know— and it's not cheating if you have an intern or assistant helping you spot opportunities to be useful, and even executing them. My interns help me make sure I never forget to do something special for people's birthdays, with a little direction from me.

What your system looks like can take so many forms. Here are some things I've seen people doing recently that deserve a little bow and a lot of copycatting:

- Give small gifts of appreciation that allow you to patronize a friend's business at the same time. This is a big one for me. When I'm considering what to get someone for their birthday, my first stop for shopping is always stores and businesses owned by friends and mentees, like Sugarwish, TomboyX, and Hanky Panky.

- Write weekly thank-you notes and year-round valentines. The product manager for the *AP Stylebook*, Colleen Newvine, does this as a Sunday hobby with her husband, and it has become as much a gratitude practice as a way of giving back.
- Write an online review for someone's business or on their LinkedIn page.
- Four times a year, post a list of businesses and products you're using and recommend, like the growth coach Charlene DeCesare does. This is generous to the businesses and to the people who might need them.
- Andy Ellwood, the cofounder of grocery app Basket, pings his network with this message every time he has a long train ride or layover: "Anything I can be helpful with? Give me a call." This last one is great because it creates a reoccurring ritual that fits into the crazy moving parts of his schedule.

Try to set aside a monthly or quarterly budget for gifts, even a tiny one. A thoughtful token—however small or silly—can be surprisingly profound, even for people who think they aren't "into" gifts (like me). A few years ago, my beautiful New York City apartment, blocks from my office at Barnard and with views of the Hudson River and Riverside Park, was destroyed by a fire. Shortly after, while I was still living out of a suitcase and reluctantly house-hunting, my friend Whitney Smith sent me a T-shirt that read POLITE AS FUCK—and yes, I have been known to wear it in public—with no return address. Getting a fresh, sassy, soft T-shirt from some anonymous benefactor crushed me, in the best possible way. When I found out it was her, I was even happier. Sometimes a little gesture is all it takes to be reminded that the only way to rise up from the ashes is to be lifted by the seeds of goodness you plant every day, inside the people who love you.

So there's the emotional case for generosity, both given and received. Here's the pragmatic one: Staying connected saves you from two productivity traps that can snare entrepreneurs. The first trap is starting to think everything is in your control; success is just a function of whether you do the work. Actually, your business will flourish only if it's a product of the hard work and intention of many. (It's hilarious that the infamous champion of capitalism, Ayn Rand, was so hung up on personal independence when I know that a business is only as successful as the strength of the community supporting its owner.)

The second trap is thinking linearly: *To solve a problem, I do* this *and then* this *and then* that, ad infinitum, until something is complete. Instead, if you make step one reaching out and asking someone who knows better, you'll immediately knock some other steps off your list—if not the entire task. Sometimes your best leapfrog to getting a problem solved is someone else's good advice. If you make a habit of giving generously of yourself, you'll find that advice and goodwill is always on the ready.

Hack 25

The Knockout Power
Compliment

I'VE COLLABORATED WITH everyone from Hillary Clinton to Lin-Manuel Miranda, and I still frequently find myself in meetings with people who make my heart skip beats. Although I've gotten pretty good at not showing it, meeting a VIP—whether a celebrity, a billionaire, or someone who has status in your bubble—is usually a tricky dynamic.

Here's the challenge. There's an instinctive impulse to be gracious and to admit to what you both know is true: In some corridor of power, they're a god or a goddess. But their status doesn't make *you* their lapdog—and if you want the relationship to continue, that's key to remember. Trust me when I tell you that they have plenty of puppy types in their life already. Fame and status can take all the oxygen out of the room, and it can be almost as suffocating for the celeb as it is for you. They're often dying for an authentic moment.

The solution is a trick—really, a social grace, not a sleight of hand—I've used hundreds of times to immediately breathe life into such an exchange and step into my own power. Give a genuine, generous compliment that shifts the balance in your favor. The mistake most people make is sharing something that makes the imbalance worse. Do it well, though, and you'll not just boost your credibility, you'll create an interaction that the person won't soon forget.

Recently, I had breakfast with the tennis legend Billie Jean King. Three years before I was born, my dad watched her win the Battle of the Sexes tennis match against Bobby Riggs on television. When I was growing up, it was his go-to story to remind me that I could do anything a boy could do. If I had just blurted out how I was *actually* feeling, I might have said something like, "Oh my god, you taught me I could do anything! I'm a huge fan! I can't believe I'm sitting here with you!"

That's a puppy-dog compliment. It gives you no power at all. I was there to pitch her on one of my portfolio companies. I *needed* power, enough power that she would believe me when I said that the investment opportunity I was putting on the table would improve women's lives so dramatically that she should help me raise $14 million.

I didn't start with a compliment at all. I had recently seen Billie Jean on a panel and knew she was the quintessential feisty contrarian. So I kicked things off by saying, "I think there are a lot of people who say that they want to invest in women, but they're all doing it wrong." She leaned right in. Then she said something to the effect of being an athlete, not an entrepreneur, and not knowing anything about business.

There was my opening. I politely interjected. "I don't know if I agree with that, Billie Jean," I said. "Artists and athletes are, by design, entrepreneurs. Look at all the ways you've capitalized on your career. From my perspective, you've been a pretty damn good entrepreneur your whole life."

Boom: a genuine power compliment. You don't manage a world-renowned tennis career without becoming among the savviest businesswomen around. But apparently she hadn't thought about it that way, and I was thrilled to be the one to tell her. So absolutely give someone you admire a compliment, but have it be one that comes from a place of power. I was implicitly saying, "Hey, I'm an expert on this; I know this space, and I'm able to see something you missed." I was no longer a supplicant; I was her peer—and maybe, in this one tiny little way, I had more clout than she did. And that makes the compliment all the more meaningful. "Wow," the recipient thinks. "I guess I can really take this one to the bank."

I love an opportunity to make someone feel good by speaking the truth, especially since so often I'm dropping tough love. But make no mistake that it's also strategic. I'm standing in my power in that moment. I've made a lasting impression.

At the end of that breakfast, Billy Jean stunned me by offering more help than I had even asked. You can never know how something will turn out in the end, but that morning, she was intrigued. Was her enthusiasm all because I whipped out a compliment? Hell no: She's interested because I put an incredible opportunity on the table. But owning my power gave me the calm and confidence to lay it out. It made her listen that much more closely. It increased the fidelity of my communication.

Whether or not you're meeting with VIPs, the time to start practicing the power compliment is now. Women are constantly in situations where they need to establish control, because the person across the table assumes their submission. Every day, find ways to power compliment someone you truly admire. The fashion designer Carrie Hammer, who you read about in hack 19, When the Bar's Low, Dance on It, has made a practice of doing it three times daily. That means she might be in her local bodega telling the cashier that his shirt has great topstitching—but hey, practice is practice! These everyday exchanges prepare her mentally so that the next time she's in a higher-pressure situation, the power compliment will roll out naturally.

One more thing: Don't push it. Until that genuine opportunity to speak truth strikes, keep your mouth shut. There's power in dishonesty, but only the repellent kind.

Hack 26

Don't Ever Be Sorry; Be Fabulous

THE POWER COMPLIMENT is a tactic that speaks to the larger challenge for women: How do you communicate power in a world that still wants its women soft and pliable, tricked out with makeup and better tuned for whispering secrets than giving commands? There's tons of information out there that can help you deal with overcoming these socialized expectations; see power posing, body language, and assertive language.

I'm a linguaphile, and I believe that words chosen carefully have power. Unfortunately, the most popular advice out there, though well meaning, has put women in a bind. Without a doubt, weak language—the constant *I'm sorry*s and *I think*s and *just*s and *a little*s—doesn't serve you in many (OK, most) business contexts. But some people seem to want to goad women into embracing the linguistic version of 1980s-style shoulder pads and assertiveness training. And on the other side, you have people who accuse you of serving the patriarchy when you tell them that "I'm sorry, I think you should invest in my business" never got anyone funded.

My alternative suggestion: Don't choose. Reject the binary, and instead work on expanding your range. It's *and*, not *or*, to use the classic improviser's rule. (And by the way, taking an improv class is a genius way to strengthen just about every communication muscle you'll need as an entrepreneur.) Being soft and gentle and welcoming and kind can be useful—so if this is you, consider these qualities respectable tools in your toolbox. I have a colleague, Jennifer Shaw, who's the exemplar of "nice" Midwestern charm. It's not my way of interacting, but I can see how well it has served not just her career but the women in her orbit. She created an entire networking community, NYTechWomen, based on leading with warmth, openness, and generosity.

Don't wait to be at the negotiating table to practice, say, strong asks. Take advantage of low-stakes business exchanges to exercise the communications muscles that are weak for you—like when you're talking to customer service about an order that got screwed up. Here's an exercise: Try calling customer service and ask questions or make complaints about any product you own. I'm not kidding. They're out there waiting for your call. Pay attention to what works when, so you can get better at shifting from gentle to firm, as situations require. It's like code switching, moving fluidly between multiple languages, dialects, or cultural norms—so if you grew up bilingual or in any kind of multicultural household, you're already a pro. When you get comfortable with that sort of flexibility, you won't need to be self-conscious anymore. You'll have built the confidence to communicate in a style that is uniquely yours.

Don't get me wrong: An *I'm sorry* tic is still indefensible. When I teach girlpreneurs at the Barnard high school summer camp, *No I'm sorry*s is the first rule that I write on the whiteboard. I like how one *New York Times* writer put it: "It's a Trojan horse for genuine annoyance, a tactic left over from centuries of [women] having to couch basic demands in palatable packages in order to get what we want. All that exhausting maneuvering is the etiquette equivalent of a vestigial tail."[1] Amen. Start any exchange with *I'm sorry* (whether it's responding to an email you've taken a day to reply to or kicking off a critique of a colleague's argument), and you've immediately handed off power.

So what is the alternative? It isn't tweezing your language until it's the equivalent of a power eyebrow. You don't want to sound like a robot. Here's what the alternative looks like for me. Recently, I dropped the ball on an email chain with a potential investor whom I met through friends in San Francisco. It had been a busy couple of weeks, and I hadn't responded to his LinkedIn connection either. Then I booked another Bay Area trip and realized it was time to reconnect. I could have started my email with "Hey, I'm so sorry I've been out of touch, things got busy." Except three things:

1. It wouldn't have been honest.
2. Why would I want to set that dynamic?
3. And finally: *BORING!*

Maya Angelou was right when she said that people won't remember what you did, they'll remember how you made them feel. So instead of *I'm sorry*, I wrote: "Hey, fabulous, how are you doing? I'm coming to San Francisco next week." It felt confident, and it felt like *me*. But I was still surprised by the enthusiastic response: "No one's ever addressed me as fabulous, but I love it. Thank you." Just that one word made it the best email he had gotten that day. He's an experienced investor type, and my guess is that few people come to him in a spirit of fun. He's used to feeling powerful, not fabulous.

We're in a moment where women and some men are *finally* speaking publicly about the sexually predatory male-dominated VC community. (Next up: everyone owning up to the problem in tech at large.) Women can feel pressured to neuter their language—their gender—so that no VC will ever mistake their intentions as anything but serious. This is understandable, but I think it's equally a wrong turn. We can't be at our most confident, which is to say our most authentic, if we're constantly policing ourselves.

Someone might say that by calling an attractive single man

whom I met in a fuzzy collegiate-social context *fabulous*, I was setting myself up for trouble. I'll own that it's *possible* that there's some part of him that wonders, maybe even hopefully, "Is she flirting with me?" But I don't worry about that, because I'm always communicating from a place of power. So while he may wonder, he's not going to assume. In fact, he'll be afraid to assume, because he knows if he's wrong, I'm going to shoot him down so fast his ego may never recover. He's a VC, after all; he knows what *too risky* looks like.

I can push these edges not because I'm so charming or bold but because I've communicated my way through so many contexts over the years. If anything, I tend toward a "no-bullshit, let's just get it done" style, and I've learned that there are times when that can actually slow things down instead of speeding things up— times when I need more of my friend Jennifer Shaw's Midwestern courtesy. If you are an empath or another "unconventional" type of leader, don't feel bad about it. Celebrate it—then practice leading with candor. I'd never ask you to take on a style that doesn't feel natural, but almost everyone can be more honest. Fundamentally, these are different cultures. And the same way you can still be you if you're parachuted into a new country, this is just about broadening your range. The goal here isn't to make you switch sides but to give you more tools for your toolbox, so that you'll be too busy being fabulous to ever be sorry.

Hack 27

Show Me the Receipts

MAYBE YOU'RE FAMILIAR with the internet meme "Show me the receipts!" It's an artifact of an old interview between Diane Sawyer and Whitney Houston. When Diane confronted Whitney with a headline saying she had spent $730,000 on drugs, Whitney wasn't having it. "I wanna see the receipts," she responded. "From the drug dealer that I bought $730,000 worth of drugs from." Despite the hilarious impossibility of receipts from a dealer (and the sad probability that the numbers were legit), Whitney was actually giving us all a useful lesson: If you want to be taken seriously, *show me the receipts*.

Any outsider who's looking to cut through the bullshit of privilege and in-group bias needs to come to the table with data that quantifies their company's success. OK, you don't need a pocketful of receipts; just specificity and care when it comes to presenting data. When you've got thoughtful numbers to show you're legit, it matters a lot less what you look like or even what language you speak. Data is the lingua franca of business. Sure, research shows[1] white men at long tables will question your data or expect it to show faster growth, a larger market, more traction, more than they might if you were someone who looked like them. But the better you get at learning to tell a compelling growth story with bulletproof evidence, the better your shot at leapfrogging their stupidest biases. It's not about spouting numbers ad infinitum. It's finding the numbers that show them you're the one who will get the results that matter—the receipts. So to speak.

Joan Fallon, the founder and CEO of Curemark, comes to mind as an incredible example of this hack in action. Curemark is poised to be the first drug on the market that will treat symptoms of autism, an illness that affects 1 in 68 school-age children, up from 1 in 150 in 2000. Joan is now widely celebrated as a pioneer and innovator. But fifteen years ago, she was a biotech outsider in every imaginable way.

For twenty-five years, she was a clinician, face-to-face with children every day as a pediatric chiropractor in the New York City area. She started noticing a pattern in the diet of her autistic patients—lots of carbs and no protein. When she spoke to MDs specializing in autism, they told her it was about mouth feel; the chewiness of protein set off sensory sensitivities typical of kids with autism. But Joan didn't buy it. She had seen how unique these sensitivities were from kid to kid, so why would so many react to this one sensation?

For eight years, she self-funded the third-party testing of these kids. Again and again the tests showed that the children who didn't eat protein (more than 60 percent of her smaller sample, and eventually a larger one) had pathologically low levels of a critical digestive enzyme in their guts. She tested these kids over and over, until she believed that even the biggest skeptic would say, "OK, this data is overwhelming. More than 60 percent of autistic kids lack an essential enzyme to digest protein." The only question then would be, "What would happen if we could synthesize that enzyme?"

Only at that moment of near irrefutability did she go out and ask for money. "It was the repeatability of that third-party testing and the overwhelming data I had collected that allowed me to leave practice and raise money. That was what gave me the confidence to do it. But what made me do it was that I was compelled—this could be helpful to children. Why would I just sit with it and not do something?"

It wasn't just Joan who was an outsider; it was her entire approach to drug development. The modern pharmaceutical industry engineers proprietary molecular compounds and only *then* looks for possible applications in patients. Crazy, right? Instead, Joan was responding directly to a demonstrated patient need. She's the living embodiment of patient-centric innovation.

Still, people pushed back. For example, one guy she pitched looked her in the face and said, "Who the hell are *you* to have discovered this?" And yet: Having the hard numbers gave her the assurance to accept her first $200,000 investment, in the form of a check written at a friend's kitchen table. (We all could use such a friend.) It also helped give her the wherewithal to say *no* when her first outside funding offer came in with predatory terms and a lot of bullying. "I can be cavalier about it today, but it was hard," she says.

That data opened many new doors once her friends and family network was tapped. She has raised more than $100 million to press forward with development of the drug, which, at the time of printing this book, has been fast-tracked for approval by the FDA pending results of the final trials.

Finding the right numbers to convey the value of your business is a slam-dunk first step; more on that in the next section, Fund. For now I want to focus on something equally important: To really land your message, numbers alone don't cut it. To open doors and minds, you need those numbers to tell a story that sticks—ideally, one that sticks so well that the person you share it with can easily pass it on to someone else.

In my network, the absolute goddess of sticky, data-backed stories is the veteran social entrepreneur Jess Weiner. As a CEO, strategist, and cultural changemaker, Jess partners with global brands to rethink how they engage with and portray women and girls. Over the course of her career, Jess has helped Dove disrupt the beauty industry with its award-winning Real Beauty campaign and worked with Mattel to reimagine Barbie's body.

"Brands are trying to do the right thing and many of them are interested in empowerment work. I'm there to help develop strategy and messaging that speaks to consumers authentically and effectively and ensures that their diverse audience is reflected," she says. "To do this successfully, I make sure to root all of my recommendations and insights in data, but we find a way to tell the story of that data in a way that can be humanized and shared," she adds. "I push my brand partners to think about the nuances of human life differently."

When Mattel brought her on, the legendary toy company knew it had a big problem. Barbie dolls aside, it was taking heat for gendered marketing. "There was a much bigger problem than everything for girls being pink," says Jess, about the pinkwashing complaint that got the most headlines. She saw that Millennial parents want their kids to be value-driven and for both girls and boys to have toys that represent the widest range of opportunities for their future identities. The problem wasn't really pink; it was toys that boxed multidimensional girls (and boys, too) into tired old gender stereotypes.

How do you make a roomful of marketing executives internalize a new idea? Jess could have handed them a ream of data and said, "Today's girls are multidimensional." But who would that excite? Nobody. Instead, she distilled the numbers into a concept with spark. "I walked in and said, 'Today's girls are *Yes, And* girls. They like pink, *and* they want to be president. They love sparkly things, *and* they love soccer.' I was marketing to the marketer, giving them a terminology and a framework to grasp it, share it, and educate their teams around it," she says.

Think of it this way: Your data needs the vehicle of story if you want people to internalize it, remember it, and repeat it. Don't just dump numbers at their feet. Put them in the context of a bite-size narrative that creates instant meaning. That's the way to have them speaking your language, long after you leave the room.

Master Startup Jedi Mind Tricks

I'M SURE YOU'VE heard a thousand times that to be persuasive, you need to build rapport. That conventional advice also happens to be sound advice: Mirror body language and energy levels, look for common ground, and you quickly set a stranger at ease. My friend and collaborator Courtney Seard, however, told me about another kind of mirroring, which I've heard a lot less about and believe is super important for anyone pitching their business. Courtney says to mirror body language, mirror energy, yes, but also mirror spoken language. If you get good at this, it can have an almost hypnotic effect. People will become more amenable to what you have to say—exactly what you need to spin a convincing growth story about the future of your company.

Courtney is an executive coach—she's worked with entrepreneurs at Richard Branson's Necker Island, for one—with an incredible energy and focus that inspired me to hire her to co-facilitate our first Galvanize training for the United State of Women. She helps people reshape the way they communicate around the way the person they're speaking to thinks. She also helps you communicate better with *yourself*, so that you can understand and tweak your own behavior in a way that will assist you in life and at work.

Let's say you're going to pitch a potential investor. You know to mirror her body language—but you also want to listen to the way she speaks. Courtney says people's words are often clues to their learning style, of which she says there are three: visual (sight); auditory (hearing); and kinesthetic (touch).

Some typical patterns:

- Visual: "I see," "It looks like"
- Auditory: "I hear you," "It sounds like"
- Kinesthetic: "I feel like"

Mirror their speech, and you'll instantly help them connect to what you're saying. But "speaking their language" isn't just linguistic. It's also about mirroring their *values* as you tell your story. With an investor, that means knowing their firm's investment thesis—the principles that guide who they choose to invest in. At BRAVA, for example, I need companies to show me that they have a high-growth business that creates measurable economic impact for women, at scale. But I'm easy—those values are baked into BRAVA's entire model. With some people, you might just have to ask.

What all this does is to create what Courtney calls *plausibility*. Are they picking up what you're putting down? Courtney told me one more way to quickly create plausibility: Use *connecting* phrases like "which means" and "because." What these and similar words do is encourage people to make connections as you speak. Pull up any political speech on YouTube and you'll see lots of examples. When you get someone to make the connection—to say to themselves, "Oh yeah, I see now what that means"—you've got them actively building the scaffolding to support your larger argument. You're laying it out for them step by step, making it all feel self-evident.

Courtney can easily spend hours talking about this. The simply takeaway truth is this: People communicate and learn in many different ways. The more conscious you are of your own patterns, and the better an observer you are of theirs, the more readily you can clear out the junk that causes perfectly reasonable people to react to others in less than rational ways—and yes, that includes gender bias. Your goal is to shape the dynamic in any room you enter, not be a victim of it.

Bring a Red-Hot Trojan Horse

BUILDING A MASSIVE, influential network becomes much easier if, every time you reach out to someone, you're galloping through their gates on a red-hot Trojan horse. That's how the punk-rock humanitarian goddess Leigh Blake put the AIDS crisis front and center in the global psyche, raising millions of dollars to fight the disease and making it a literal cause célèbre, with Bono most famously carrying the banner. Later she recruited Alicia Keys as her cofounder in Keep a Child Alive, which has provided life-saving AIDS drugs, care, and support to hundreds of thousands of children and families in Africa and India.

No one can be as cool, or as *mega*, as Leigh Blake, to use one of her favorite words. This woman is the definition of *badass*. But we *can* learn to be almost as crafty in how we approach new contacts and always gallop in with a red-hot ask: one that is concrete, appealing to the other person's self-interest, and sexy—which, of course, means different things to different people.

So let's talk about Leigh. First, she's a leapfrogger. She's Cockney British, born in the projects ("council flats"). When she got kicked out of school at sixteen, she followed her passion—music—by following The Who around England. She made her way to the

States as a writer and photographer and became a fixture in the late-'70s punk scene centered around New York's CBGB nightclub.

Leigh says she's not an entrepreneur. I say she is. When she decided to devote her career to fighting AIDS, first in the United States and then in Africa, she took on the hardest challenge of entrepreneurship there is: educating a market. This was the late '80s. Leigh's circle of musicians and artists in New York City had been devastated by the HIV virus, but most Americans were oblivious or uninterested. AIDS was the "gay disease," not *their* problem.

Leigh and her friend John Carlin, an entertainment lawyer, had an idea: What if they could change the way Americans—and, for that matter, the gay community— thought about AIDS by sneaking the message in on the red-hot Trojan horse of pop culture?

Carlin had the perfect horse. His law firm represented the estate of Cole Porter, an American legend. So John and Leigh decided they'd record a charity album, with rock stars reinterpreting Cole Porter classics. They'd call it *Red Hot + Blue*, after the composer's 1936 Broadway musical. It would all be pro bono—a big deal since it wasn't yet a "thing" for musicians to devote their time and fame currency to giving back. "When you come to people in the entertainment industry and you say, 'I want gifts of the things that you would generally employ to make millions,' I think it's actually much harder than starting a business, because ultimately there's no [money in it] for the person that you are persuading, generally a money-hungry manager or agent," says Leigh.

Leigh didn't have a hundred famous rock stars to call, but she did have one: her old buddy David Byrne. When she explained the concept of the album, he immediately said yes. At that moment, David became the patron saint of *Red Hot*.

Now she had two horses in the stable: Cole Porter and David Byrne. At that point it was easy to sign on musicians, Bono included, because everyone wanted to be associated with David, who had just appeared on the cover of *Time* magazine. (When it came to getting ABC to air the concert, the deal was also a Trojan horse: "We told them the money was going to help people with AIDS, but we never told them that the entire program would be a ninety-minute safe-sex, anti-discrimination manifesto.") It was a huge hit, selling more than one million copies and raising millions of dollars for AIDS organizations. The Red Hot organization went on to produce nineteen more charity albums.

Again and again Leigh has used this concept to persuade artists and their gatekeepers to join her effort. Here's why people say yes to her:

- **The brand is sexy:** "People look at my work, and it doesn't look like charity work. It doesn't look earnest, like it was created by suits at the UN. It doesn't look middle-aged. It really does look very rock and roll."
- **She's all-in, all the time:** "They want someone who's so passionate that they feel comfortable that that person will never kind of let it crash and burn to the ground. And that hopefully, when that manager learns more, because you've managed to attract them, you get more airtime to really give them the details that they can then sell to their artist."
- **She makes it clear what's in it for them:** "What is it that would take this artist to a next-level place that would be really, really inspiring for them and that would be equal to the work that they generally do? It's compassionate, it's glossy, and it's well-produced. When you convince them of that, you're on the road to success."

How do you put this to work to build your own network and raise awareness around what you're up to? It's not like you could create a star-studded charity album. (Or could you? Leigh hadn't, until she had.) If you look around, you'll see Trojan horses all the time. There's a reason that people won't write a $500 check to a charity but will write a $1,000 check for a place at the table at a charity gala, where they'll have an excuse to dress up and be photographed and—the most important part—clink glasses with other people who paid $1,000.

At the most basic level, be thoughtful anytime you meet someone new: What will show them you're legit and of interest to them? What is *their* idea of sexy? You want people to see that a connection to you will pay off—not necessarily in dollars but in enjoyment, fun, meaning, *anything* that you can uniquely, authentically bring to the table.

Sometimes a Trojan horse is a simple matter of language. When we launched Nely Galán's book *Self Made*, we avoided the word *entrepreneurship*—even though it's more than two hundred pages devoted to helping women start small businesses and the word appears frequently throughout. We felt that we needed to sneak that advice inside approachable language, and *entrepreneurship* is a word that scares off beginners. It sounds lofty and removed, particularly if you're spending your days, say, punching register buttons, remote from the world depicted in *Fast Company* and *TechCrunch*. *Self-made*, meanwhile, carries with it a tangible, inspiring sense of possibility for everyone. The research clearly told us a story: Use *entrepreneurship*, and lots of folks will feel as though it's not for them. So the title, *Self Made*, became Nely's Trojan horse. Some might call that a bait and switch. I prefer to call it a Trojan horse, because in the war of ideas, creativity wins. And if what's inside is of value to your customer, who cares how you got it to them, as long as they're happy and your business is growing.

SECTION 4

Fund

Investment is overrated. Your best chance for success is a business model that's bringing in revenue from day 1 and profitable ASAP. So before you think about finding capital, think about how to increase revenue and decrease costs so that you can be your own number one investor.

Still the moment will come: You'll need money. I mentioned earlier that I left academia after realizing that what's really holding women back isn't a lack of education, it's access to capital. At some point even the scrappiest of scrappy founders find themselves bumping into that stupidly true cliché: *You've got to spend money to make money.* Thankfully, there are many players now in the arbitrage game of finding the talent missed by traditional investors, including dozens of funds focused on women-led businesses, as well as a few to support people of color. The Wharton School has produced a global compendium of gender-lens investors called Project Sage, available online.

But as I see it, before the access gap, there's an awareness gap. I know MBAs who are lost when it comes to understanding, let alone tapping, the landscape of fundraising opportunities—but they have networks to lean on to sort out the basics and understand where they fit in. If you, like most people, don't have that network ready to answer your questions, this section is your guide through the carnival funhouse of funding your business.

Hack 30

Funding 101: Start Scrappy, Stay Scrappy

HERE'S THE THING about startup capital: It's expensive. You either pay interest, or you give away a chunk of your company or its future profits. Before you do either, push bootstrapping to its maximum limits. Clean house by making sure every cost is not only accounted for but likely to pay for itself in future returns. Women, especially those who have ever run a household, don't need a lecture on how to stretch the value of their dollars. That said, here are three opportunities I see many entrepreneurs consistently missing out on.

1. **Don't buy or rent anything—until you've first asked to have it for free.** My first business, which cracked my world wide open, started with the simple trade I shared earlier. I built a website, got a car. Did I abandon this MO when budgets got bigger? No way. Every new business has to start scrappy. Right now, for example, I'm thinking about how I can get BRAVA some additional free office space in Manhattan, one of the tightest real estate markets in the country.

   If you want free stuff, make asking a habit. Ask, ask, ask. Most women (and plenty of men) need to ask more and ask *for* more. I listened recently to a TED Talk in which an entrepreneur named Jia Jiang talked about his self-improvement project: Over one hundred days, he made one hundred ridiculous requests of strangers—things he was sure people would say no to. At a burger joint, for example, he asked the cashier, "Can I have a refill on my burger?" At a Krispy Kreme donut shop, he asked the woman at the counter if she could sell him a box of donuts refashioned into the Olympic symbol of interlocking colored rings. The crazy thing was that about half the time, people said yes! (Burger guy said no. Donut lady said yes.)

People in the U.S. spend too much time in Big Retail and therefore don't haggle much. As a result, we've lost sight of the fact that everything is a negotiation. We also overemphasize the currency of money. This hack isn't really about getting things for free; it's learning to work in alternative currencies. Mine is usually my network. When I meet with someone from the co-working space I have my eye on for BRAVA, my open won't be, "Hey, how about some free space?" I'll offer to organize a quarterly event, drawing on my ability to quickly amass an interesting group of people who'll draw attention to the space and create an opportunity for current tenants to make connections and build their community. These events might even directly result in new memberships. I'll ask them what that's worth to them—a desk? An office? Maybe start with a four-month lease and see how it goes? (Update: I scored an offer for free space in SoHo; now I have to decide if I still want it.)

Your currency might be your network. Or it might be exposure; association with your brand; a philanthropic opportunity; a chance for market research, knowledge exchange, audience development, or shelf space—anything. Mutual interest is like working with pieces of a puzzle, and as you train your mind, you get better and better at spotting the complementary edges.

2. **The website is dead.** Tell me how an entrepreneur spends their first $1,000, and I'll tell you whether they're going to be successful. It's like the Magic 8 Ball of startups. If, for example, I hear that someone's first $1,000 is spent on their website, nine times out of ten, "My sources say no."

One of my BRAVA advisors, Eason Jordan, ran a media company called NowThis News after leaving his executive role at CNN. They made big headlines during the 2016 election because they got so many eyeballs on their videos. Their livestream of the third presidential debate was second in viewership only to ABC News. A four-year-old company beat major networks!

When Jordan first mentioned NowThis to me, I had never heard of it. "It's news for Millennials," he told me.

"Oh, cool," I said. "What's the website?"

"We don't *do* websites anymore, Nathalie," he told me. "Nobody's going to go to a browser and say, 'Let me go to nowthisnews.com and go get my news from there.' That's just not a thing. That's not going to happen." (Fortunately, Eason's older than me. Someone younger probably would have finished by asking if I needed a parking space for my walker.)

NowThis News does have a website. Until a 2018 upgrade, the homepage read, "HOMEPAGE. EVEN THE WORD SOUNDS OLD. WE BRING THE NEWS TO YOUR SOCIAL FEED," and linked out to their social feeds—at least nine Facebook pages, two Twitter handles, three Instagram channels, a YouTube channel, and a Snapchat account. While the site may now have more features, I'm betting the social feeds are still where the eyeballs are.

I don't think NowThis News or media in general is an outlier in this shift. Abandoning the classic website—or at least putting it on your "nice to have" list as you prioritize spending—makes old-fashioned business sense. When you're introducing your customers to something new in the marketplace, you don't ask your customers to go to you. You go to your customer, whether that means getting a board game into Starbucks or moderating a Facebook page.

Just to be clear: Saying you don't need a website is very different from saying you don't need to be online. Of *course* you need to be online. You need to be wherever your customers are, *online*. But instead of a website, you might have a Facebook page with an option to sign up for an email newsletter. You might have a Yelp page and incentivize customers to write reviews. You might set yourself up on Etsy. You'll have as many outposts as your customers frequent.

I've met so many people in the earliest days of their business who are obsessively (and often expensively) building their websites. Most of them would have been much better off spending that time and energy on figuring out how to connect to their customer more directly. I get it: Giving your business a virtual home makes it feel more real, and tangible— even to yourself. It's a public declaration—the digital equivalent of hanging your shingle, whether you have any customers yet or not.

Well, I'm sorry to break it to you, darling. You're a business owner now. The time for sentimentality is someday in the far future, when you're swimming in twelve feet of money. Today, how strategically you spend your limited capital—cash, but also attention capital—can decide whether you're still here in three years, let alone thirty. If you really want an official "stamp" for your business, spend the twelve to fifteen dollars and buy your URL (mycompanyname. com), then have it forward visitors to wherever your clients go most, like your Etsy or Facebook page, for example. That way your business cards or email signature can still have a nice and easy-to-remember URL featured.

That said, by all means build a custom website for your new business, *if and only if* you can make a strong case that it is the best, fastest, cheapest way to accomplish a specific goal you have for your business in the next year. And even then, build it cheap. In fact, apply that test any time you're considering a spend.

3. **Don't pay for paid interns.** Anybody looking to scale a capital-constrained business needs interns. What they lack in experience, they make up for in smarts, hunger, and flexibility. But those interns need to be paid. If they're not, it's bad for them, bad for you, bad for your brand, and bad for social mobility. In the past couple of years, everyone from Oprah to Lena Dunham to Hillary Clinton has eaten crow for using unpaid talent. After a five-year legal battle, Fox Searchlight settled with two interns who worked for free in the production office of *Black Swan*.

Bottom line, it's not cool, it puts you in legally sketchy territory, and it eliminates people who can't afford to work for free from your potential candidate pool—folks who might have been the smartest, scrappiest members of your team. Meanwhile, if you treat interns well—which obviously is about much more than what you pay them—you create allies for life. I have former interns who, years later, off on their own, are still my eyes and ears. Some of my best introductions have been from former interns now perched in important places.

Yes, interns should be paid. But here's the crafty leapfrog: Why should *you* be the one paying them? At the Athena Center, we have a program called Athena Fellows, where we sponsor a student who otherwise couldn't afford to take on an unpaid or low-pay summer internship. They get a stipend, student housing, and weekly mentorship to support them during the summer internship of their choice. If I were starting a business, I'd research the academic institutions in my area (even high schools), looking for a similar program. If they don't have one, I'd approach administrators about creating one: "Hey, why don't you start a program to fund your best and brightest? And I'll take three interns, please." Introduce them to Athena Fellows as a model. Universities increasingly understand that they're not preparing kids for the workforce if they graduate them without work experience, and they have resources to devote to that effort. Doing the legwork to establish a program will take an investment of time, but if it creates a steady stream of subsidized interns over the next many semesters, it'll be well worth it.

MICROHACK

Interns Are for Intel

I would like to be able to do all the background research that allows me to be thoughtful and personal in every meeting I have, but there are only twenty-four hours in the day. Interns bridge the gap. When I meet with someone new, my intern researches the contact and their company, finding everything publicly available and of interest. That way, five minutes before a meeting I can open the dossier and have the 411 to strike up a meaningful conversation and be respectful of our time together.

Hit leapfroghacks.com/dossier to get my research template and read an actual dossier an intern put together for me.

Hack 31

Raise Prices, Stat

WHEN ENTREPRENEURS NEED to get more money in the door, raising prices is often one of the easiest solutions. Why do so many run screaming from it? I am willing to bet that whatever it is you do, whatever it is you sell, you're currently charging too little. Likewise, for those who are already fundraising, you're probably not asking for enough. Just as in salary negotiations, women routinely ask for less than men. When I asked Joan Fallon of Curemark what she had learned from multiple rounds of fundraising, her quick answer was: "You always need more than you think." Think like a project manager, who always builds in an additional 25 percent buffer because, well, stuff happens.

It's a given that you're conscientious and exacting when it comes to the quality of your offering; you have to be. So allow yourself to switch your attention for a moment to the psychology of pricing. Being savvy about how to use every variable to your advantage is part of the game of business. Ignore the psychological game, and you're shortchanging yourself.

Does quality drive pricing? Meh. Quality is just one factor that determines how much you can charge, and it's maybe not even the most important. A friend once chatted up a guy on Long Island who owned a limo company. He told her that a few years back, he had expanded business into the Hamptons, the string of famous beaches where New York's 1 percenters spend their summer weekends. First he ran an ad identical to the one he used in less-ritzy corners of Long Island. No one booked. After doing some research, he ran the same ad—but increased the price 80 percent. Right away, the phone started ringing.

Same product, same service, two very different price points. That's just an anecdote. There are *hundreds* of studies out there about the crazy psychology of pricing. In his book *Predictably Irrational*, Dan Ariely writes about an experiment he ran using a subscription offer for *The Economist*. He offered one hundred MIT students three options: a one-year $59 digital subscription, a $125 print subscription, or $125 print + digital subscription. Nobody chose the print-only option; eighty-four people chose print + digital. Ariely then took another one hundred students, and this time he offered just two options: $59 for digital or $125 for print. This time, the numbers swung the other way—most of the students went for the $59 digital subscription. That middle option, it turned out, helped convince the students that the most expensive offering was also the best deal. Marketing experts call that a *decoy*.

You've probably experienced this phenomenon yourself. Have you noticed that in nice restaurants, menus hardly ever have a dollar sign anymore? It's just *Scallops with parsnips–24* or *Octopus salad–19*. That's because studies have shown people spend more when they don't have to think about that ugly dollar sign, which makes them think about their credit card bill, which in turn makes them think about the consequence of a dinner that's six dollars a bite.

Yet another big variable: context. If you've ever been caught in a rainstorm in Manhattan, you know that you'll happily spend twenty dollars on the world's crappiest umbrella because there's a guy on the corner who was smart enough to be there when you needed him.

There are all kinds of reasons why aspiring leapfroggers, and particularly women, ask for too little, financial behaviorist Jacquette M. Timmons tells me. Jacquette has worked with upwards of a thousand women entrepreneurs, either one-on-one or in groups, to tease out the emotional side of money management—and that definitely includes pricing strategy. She says the problem of women lowballing themselves is rampant. Too many entrepreneurs suffer from *scarcity mind-set*, the belief that the world's financial pie is finite and there's not enough for everybody. That mind-set is at odds with history; our economy has been growing, aside from a handful of blips, since 1934. While we could argue about whether we pay *too* much attention to economic growth at the cost of other good things like the health of the planet or the health of our neighbors, the fact is, the pie has been getting bigger.

So let's all do our part to increase the national GDP by raising our prices. According to Jacquette, the following are among the most common stumbling blocks.

- **You entangle pricing with self-worth.** People who've grown up with financial insecurity sometimes have trouble thinking they're "worth" high prices. Take yourself out of the equation and focus on your product or service. Many businesspeople mistakenly approach pricing as an equation of cost of material plus the value of their own time. Instead, they should focus on how much value it has to the *customer.* Jacquette says, "Shift attention to what you've created, whether it's a service or a product or a hybrid. *Here's the problem that it's solving for people, and it's valued at X.* That's a much less emotional equation than saying to yourself, 'I'm gonna charge what I'm worth.'" In other words, try to quantify how much value your product or service is creating for the user. What goal is it helping them achieve that they couldn't, or couldn't as quickly, without your help and support? Will it save or earn them money over time? How much—and what percentage of that should go into your pocket?

■ **You confuse your own shopping habits with your customers'.** If you've spent a lifetime shopping with low price as your top priority, you might assume everyone else shops that way, too. In fact, there are people who will turn their nose up at a product that's priced too low. (See Mr. Limousine at the beginning of this hack.) You may be in a market where price matters a lot, but make sure you're arriving at your conclusion using research to complement gut intuition.

■ **You worry your existing customers will decamp.** Some of them may. A better strategy in many cases is pricing high to start and then decreasing it over time as you scale up and gain efficiency. But if you've started with your prices too low to make that possible, or are in a service business where increasing prices is part of your strategy, your best chance to retain people is in communicating up front. "Give them a heads-up that pricing is going up to X. Even if you choose to grandfather them into the lower price, you should let them know prices have increased for everyone else. Otherwise, choose a time frame—say, three or six months—and let them know that's when prices will increase," says Jacquette. I'll take that one step further: If you exempt someone from your increased rates, let them know that they're special—make them feel good about why they're getting the deal. Even better, make them feel grateful, so that they'll respond well when you also let them know that you'd greatly appreciate their help in the form of promotion or referrals.

If conversations about money give you the shakes, prepare ahead of time. Jacquette says, "Stick with the facts. If you need to write yourself a script so that you can address the nervous energy that may come up, then do that, but just don't feel like you have to justify it. 'The price is going up. This is when it's gonna happen.' There you go."

- **You worry you won't find customers who can afford you.** It's true that raising prices might require you to make changes to other aspects of your strategy—namely, where you're finding your customers. You may need to change your advertising, marketing, or distribution. You may need to tweak the product. But don't make the mistake of thinking the customer who will pay more simply isn't out there. Jacquette sees a lot of women with the mentality, "If I charge X, I might not get enough customers, so let me play it safe and charge the lower amount." But think of it this way: If you charge more, you can afford to have a smaller customer base, and you'll have more time to work on growing the business.

There's one positive in the messy commingling of emotions and money. Says Jacquette, "Underpricing yourself does even more damage to you emotionally and psychically than it does to your bottom line." So be generous and examine every option when it comes to giving yourself—and your business—a raise. When you take a stand for your product or service by raising prices and get the *yes* nod from the market, the emotional benefit is off the charts.

Hack 32

#$@! The "Friends and Family" Round

NEED PROOF THAT the mainstream game of entrepreneurship is rigged? Look no further than the infamous "Friends and Family" round. Here's how AngelBlog.net defines it: "Friends and Family financings are always *the easiest to complete*—often taking less than two months from start to finish. Friends and Family rounds usually raise $25,000 to $150,000 in total—*the amount depends a lot on who your friends and family are.*" (The italics I added as eye rolls.)

The app-turned-fintech entrepreneur Sheena Allen put it to me well: "We go talk to investors, and they tell me, 'Oh, you should just raise a family and friends round,'" she says. "I'm like, I don't know about your family and friends, but most of my family and friends are probably asking *me* for money, not giving me money."

The privilege baked into this model is ludicrous and makes it difficult for anyone without wealthy friends and family to ever receive investment capital. This absurdity came up recently on a panel, and after I called bull, an older, white gentleman stepped up to explain why, really, it wasn't about privilege at all. "You have to understand where these investors are coming from," he said.

"They want to see that you believe enough in your business to have invested your own nest egg. They want to see that you have taken the trouble to go to your community and family and ask them to put skin in the game. They want to see that the people who know you are excited. It's a form of traction."

This guy couldn't even comprehend the possibility of living in a world where your family would literally do *anything* to make you successful—and yet are totally without the resources to monetize their love and enthusiasm. And by the way, even people whose families have very limited resources often *do* raise money from friends and family—it just doesn't add up to the tens of thousands of dollars of capital that gets a business to the point where angels and seed investors will take interest. Take Sheena Allen. Between her father and an aunt and uncle, she raised about $6,000—enough to get started but nowhere near enough to grow.

Recently I spoke to a doctor who was trying to raise seed. You might think, "Oh, a doctor, she must have the network to draw real capital and nest egg to boot." Yes, she is a physician, educated at top universities. She's also now practicing at a clinic in a tough area of Washington, DC, and struggling to pay off her student loans. Her friends and family aren't well-to-do. She believes in her business as much as anyone could—but there's no money to put in the pot. End of story.

So screw the friends and family round, and don't let yourself be flustered or think you're "less than" if you can't raise one. Instead, get out there and find what Nely Galán calls the "hidden money all over America." Nely has published a list of some of the best accelerators, grants, and contests created specifically to address this rigged game (check out becomingselfmade.com). Not only can winning a grant get you dollars and connect you to mentors and future investors, it provides that "traction" my fellow panelist spoke of—proof that someone smart was willing to back your idea with money. (More on traction soon.)

Here's another potentially deep-pocketed "friend": your local

Small Business Administration. Take advantage of every resource they have to offer. The SBA has programs to help women-run startups get early-stage bank loans. Traditionally, banks don't invest in startups. A bank makes its decisions based on their evaluation of the business *you already have*. "We take the lowest-risk clients," Gladys Preciado, a VP and senior business relationship manager at Wells Fargo told me, "because we just don't make that big of a margin on the risk that we take. They're already three years in business when they come to a bank." However, banks do make some startup loans in partnership with the SBA—because the federal government guarantees part of the loan, reducing the bank's risk. That's why working with your local SBA is so important.

Gladys told me the story of an entrepreneur she was able to help years ago, back when she was a loan officer at a small bank. She had come to Gladys, asking for $150,000 to launch her first frozen yogurt shop. Normally, Gladys's bank, like most banks big and small, required an entrepreneur to have between 25 and 50 percent of the total capital needed to get their business up and running the first year—"sort of like a down payment on a car or home," Gladys explained to me. "We typically need them to demonstrate this via a bank statement verifying the funds are available to be used toward this project."

This woman and her partner had basically no money, but they had an amazing business proposal. They had analyzed frozen yogurt shops and learned that the magic bullet for success was the self-serve model, where customers walk in and get a cup and pull the handle and add the toppings on their own.

The would-be shop owners had also done something else right: They had created a strong relationship with their local SBA. In fact, it was the SBA that first called Gladys, urging her to take the meeting and extend a loan offer. And because of all the workshops the pair took there, they had a really tight business plan. Gladys was impressed and believed they would succeed. So she thought about how they might scrape together the 25 percent capital requirement. In the end, she was able to convince her bosses that their credit card *availability* plus what little cash they had would serve as their official skin in the game. We've all heard of entrepreneurs financing their businesses (or some critical investment) on credit cards. But this is far better. *Availability* means she didn't actually have to draw the money on the credit card. She just had to show she had cards adding up to $35,000 in available credit. So she got her loan and the yogurt shop opened—and now, many years later, has become a global franchise operation with more than five hundred locations.

MICROHACK

Swipe Right (on Loan Officers)

Think about finding a loan officer like finding a spouse. What are the chances you'll find the right match with the very first person you go out with? Close to zilch. Start to think of rejection as the norm, not the sign of doom. Also consider this: When you're dating, you're not necessarily ready to get married. But you're learning along the way. Likewise, a loan officer might tell you that you're premature in your readiness for a loan—and then give you a great consultation that helps you make the next right step.

Once you do find a match, make the loan officer your partner. They're there for you, and they have a lot more to offer than just the loan. They can open their networks—for example, by introducing you to a great lawyer. They can give you advice gleaned from seeing hundreds of others start a business. Find someone who's responsive and makes time for you. It's their job to make you succeed. If they're not really working for you, go find someone who will.

Hack 33

Venture Is a White-Collar Drug

RIGHT NOW THERE'S a huge push to get businesses owned by women and people of color access to VC funding. This is great news, except for one thing: For the vast majority of businesses, and the vast majority of spending needs, venture money is a bad fit. Actually, it's a terrible fit.

These days, no doubt thanks to headlines about unicorns and multimillion-dollar rounds, everyone seems to think the brass ring is venture capital. But venture capitalists take a huge chunk of the ownership of your business (equity) and put you into a machine that is focused on one thing: exiting, which means creating returns for the investor either by selling the business or taking it public. If you're more interested in building a "forever" business than in accommodating someone else's exit strategy, venture capital might not be for you—and so it's particularly important to understand the broader picture of investment and financing.

Too many entrepreneurs, encouraged by well-meaning folks, are rushing down the equity-investment route without knowing whether it's appropriate or how the money should be used. As a result, you've got founders burning through VC funding just to keep up with operating costs. Heads up: You should never give away a piece of your company just to keep the lights on. Equity-based investment should be used to fuel growth—for example, to buy a new warehouse that will hold enough product to take you from local to regional.

Don't be sucked in by the flashy mystique of venture capital. Pursue every other alternative before you hand off ownership—even a slice of it—to a bunch of guys (or even gals) who live in an echo chamber and will do whatever it takes to push you toward an exit.

Your business may never capture a VC's interest. The vast majority of these investors are hunting for companies that have the potential to sell for ten to forty times (aka *10x to 40x*) the investment cost, rapidly. That's why tech companies, which can scale their perceived value quickly, get most of their attention and dollars. Meanwhile, non-tech companies that could provide incredible returns get ignored. As the entrepreneur and VC Kanyi Maqubela wrote recently, poking at the disturbing question of why new business formation is at a forty-year low, "Valuations have been blown out of proportion among 'fundable' companies, while those with promising but early trajectories, those with ambitious but workmanlike metrics, are perennially struggling to raise capital."[1]

Arlan Hamilton is a badass seed investor. She was sleeping on the floor at the airport and on friends' couches to scrape by when smarts, persistence, and hundreds of phone calls resulted in the first investor in her fund, Backstage Capital. Backstage invests solely in women-, people of color-, and LGBT-led businesses and has backed more than sixty companies with nearly $3 million in funding.

Arlan put the irrational exuberance around VC money this way: "VC has been looked at as an oasis in the desert. It's been made to seem so important by young, straight, white males. It becomes a little bit like a drug, and you keep needing another hit to keep the high. Women and people of color are naturally saying,

'OK, I need money to grow, I must need what they have.' What they don't realize is that they have innately what these guys are trying to achieve artificially. They're trying to raise money to bulk up their value—but actually we have that secret sauce, that magic that they're trying to acquire. It's like when people try to tan, or get lip or butt injections—they're trying to accomplish what we already have. So before you go out to raise, think about what success is. Are you going after it because you think you're supposed to or because it's really the right thing to do? Can you do with $50K what others do with $500K? Most of the time the answer is yes."

One final caveat: Don't even think about VC unless you're willing to become the minority owner of your own company. That would mean that someone besides you controls the future of your business. In fact, they could decide that the business is better off without you. Not cool? Then read on, and get to know the alternatives. There may be equity investment in your future yet, but don't mistake it for the brass ring.

MICROHACK

The Investment Cycle

Very young businesses come to me all the time looking for seed funding without understanding that BRAVA invests in companies that are already on solid footing and looking to grow. Here's a thumbnail view, drawing on a few popular sources such as Investopedia, on the life cycle of typical equity investment to help you understand where you might fit. In practice, the fundraising journey varies wildly by industry and by business and fluctuates over time, so don't take anything in this table as gospel.

Funding Round	Company Snapshot	Financial View
ANGEL	Earliest stage, money to build product or prototype	$100 to $500,000 raised; terms vary wildly
SEED	Early stage, money to build product and launch	$500,000 to $2 million raised; founder typically owns 75 to 90 percent of her company
SERIES A	Already earning revenue or has a clear plan to monetize existing users, along with a clear plan for sustainable growth; now optimizing product and growing customer base	$2 million to $15 million raised; founder typically owns 50 percent of her company
SERIES B	Upleveling the business with massive expansion of market reach; typically a new round of hires are needed to expand sales, marketing, and business development, along with operations such as customer service	$7 million to $10 million raised; founder typically owns 40 percent of her company
SERIES C	Growing, healthy business ready to scale even wider, possibly acquiring competitors	$1 million to $100 million+ raised; founder typically owns 30 percent of her company or less

Hack 34

Debt Isn't a Four-Letter Word

MOST PEOPLE HEAR the word *debt* and think, "Something I want to get out of." Get over it. If you're a woman looking for capital, debt might be your new best friend. It may not be sexy like venture, but remember: You and your business already have the secret sauce—*you*. What you need is money, and debt is the most overlooked, poorly understood capital leapfrog there is.

I recently met a passionate African American financier named Donray Von. He spent twenty years in the music industry working with artists like OutKast, Cody ChesnuTT and The Roots, then transitioned into tech investments after spending time in Silicon Valley doing one of the world's first ring-tone music licensing deals. "Tech allowed me to see how properly funded businesses were structured," Donray says. Then he met a musician whose father was billionaire Bill Gross, who at the time was running the investment firm PIMCO, managing $1.7 trillion in assets. "I went into business with his family office, partnering on a venture fund, and that experience exposed me to various funding mixes of equity, debt, and sub debt, along with structures for small- and medium-sized enterprises. Additionally, I saw firsthand the importance of an advisory board to guide founders through the maze of a growing business," says Donray.

Donray is convinced that lack of knowledge about debt is a fast-approaching train wreck for businesses owned by women and people of color, with well-meaning VCs wearing the conductor's cap. He says that young startups need to protect their *runway*, the number of months they can survive on existing cash. To finance growth, they should take on debt—but they don't, because they either think they can't get it or don't realize they need to. So for example, a small business might shoulder the expense of onboarding a big new client or customer instead of approaching a creditor for debt capital.

"Taking on debt cuts into margins, but it's a safer approach," says Donray. "Say an entrepreneur believes they have eighteen months of runway, but then they use some of that money to onboard that new client. Suddenly, the typical missteps involved in figuring out every new business become death. Because if something goes wrong, you don't have the runway you need to fix it. You can easily wake up one day out of money and out of business."

Project out a few years, and Donray is worried the business community will use such failures to draw wrongheaded conclusions about underrepresented founders. "I've seen how this movie ends," he says. "Ten years from now someone looks at the stats for women- and minority-owned businesses and says, 'They fail more than the rest,' and it will be because everyone told them to get VC money and no one assisted them in adding debt alongside of it. The failure of these businesses will create what I call a false negative. We have to do something about it."

Donray, who's had four exits as a technology investor, is doing his part by founding a company called Currency, which prepares women- and minority-owned businesses for debt and investment from family offices, banks, and institutional investors, and then gets the deals done. His final message to founders: "Try not to touch the runway. Debt is a better option for growth—and by the way, maybe debt becomes a lot more friendly a concept if we call it *credit*." (There's a bonus hack right there.)

Erin Andrew is a lender at Live Oak Bank, which is the number one SBA lender in the country, financing small businesses in more than sixteen different industries. Erin works with small firms doing business in the federal contracting space. Like Donray, she sees how equity has eclipsed debt (aka credit) in the conversation about how to close the capital gap. "There are sometimes more doors available in the debt space than in equity. But entrepreneurs think, 'I don't have capital, I don't have anything that's worth anything now, debt isn't an option.' The trouble is that folks don't understand debt well enough to leverage it." Here are the three things Erin and I want you to know about debt.

1. **Acquisition is a capital double whammy.** With Erin's help, an army veteran with an IT contracting firm was able to get a loan to acquire a $4 million business with only $25,000 of his own money. Say what?!

   When you acquire a business, Erin explains, you now have the entire cash flow of that business at your disposal. What you do with that cash is up to you. You can invest it in that company; you can invest it in your original company. Either way, it'll allow you to grow and have more control over what that growth looks like.

   It also immediately makes you more creditworthy, which is why the army veteran needed so little of his own money to access millions in financing. Also, by leveraging lending programs like the SBA's 7(a) program, entrepreneurs aren't required to put as much cash down, allowing them to leverage the cash they have for larger deals. When Erin, with the help of the SBA, considers granting a loan, she doesn't take only a balance sheet into account—she takes any *acquisitions*, *specifically the balance sheet of the company you're looking to buy,* into account as well. When it comes to lending, you're now in an entirely different weight class. "Women are decades behind in business because capital hasn't been available to us. How do we buy back those decades? Through acquisition. That's where you find the cash to grow fast," she says.

So keep your eyes open for companies or competitors that could make your own businesses stronger. Don't assume, at the start, that anything is out of your league. There are lenders who can boost your buying power.

2. **Know when you need short-term versus long-term financing.** Recently Erin helped a woman who needed $1.2 million to take on a contract opportunity, with the majority—$800,000—to be spent in one month. Her local bank suggested a long-term loan. "The products she was looking at were ten-year term loans when she only had a ten-month need," Erin says. She was able to direct her to a short-term loan product that saved her $90,000. "If she had taken out a long-term loan, she would have had her assets tied up for ten years," making it harder to get another loan.

3. **Bankers can educate you—to a point.** Your banker should be a helpful source of information, but some are trying to sell certain loan products or services. It's important to understand their commission and incentive structure. "You get terms and fine print thrown at you, and there's not enough education to really know your best option," Erin warns. Before you take out a loan, visit women's business centers and tap the resources of the local SBA. Find a counselor whose only goal is to educate you on every option out there, and shop around to make sure you've found the best loan partner. Your banker should provide you not only with capital, but also with value add advice and long-term strategic solutions to help your business grow.

MICROHACK

Give Small Banks a Big Look

Small banks that work with the SBA can be an excellent resource when you're almost ready for seed capital and your friends and family have empty pockets. These banks need your business. If you're looking for what's known as a *policy exception*—banking language for bending their own rules—a loan officer at a small bank has a lot more time to focus on your story and business and be resourceful about finding ways to get you the money you need.

Hack 35

Win the Crowd

CROWDFUNDING—ALL TYPES—SEEMS to be the one area in which women are more successful at raising money than men. Two Wharton professors looking at 1,250 Kickstarter campaigns found that women were 13 percent more likely to meet their goals.[1] And CircleUp, an equity crowdfunding platform focused on retail and consumer products, reported that in 2015, women on the site took 34 percent of the capital but were 32 percent of the total applicants for funding.[2]

Crowdfunding has grown to mean a few different things. First, there was only rewards-based crowdfunding, like Kickstarter, where "the crowd" is donating rather than investing, often in exchange for some perk—for example, early access to the product or a discounted price. But there's another option for cash-strapped entrepreneurs: equity crowdfunding. It became legal in the United States in 2016, when President Obama signed the Jumpstart Our Business Startups (JOBS) Act. For a fee, equity crowdfunding platforms connect startups with individual and sometimes institutional investors who pool their money to fund them. Sometimes they do this in exchange for equity, but more often, they get their loan repaid with interest. (Technically this is called *debt crowd-funding*, but it is readily available on equity platforms.)

Another great thing about crowdfunding is that you set the terms, and they're likely to be a lot better than what an angel or seed investor has to offer. Emily Best is an expert. She's the founder of Seed&Spark, a crowdfunding site for film entrepreneurs that has the highest campaign success rate in the world. Even better, she funded her business with the help of two crowd-funding campaigns. She tried traditional fundraising, pitching to a VC that she considered her "dream investor," but when the offer came in, her lawyer told her they were the worst terms he'd ever seen. "This is not a term sheet you counter," he told her. "This is a term sheet you go say, 'Go eff yourself.'" So she turned her back on venture and took her pitch to Crowdfunder, an equity crowd-funding site, where she set her own terms. Instead of trading equity for cash, she went after debt. Soon she had investors everywhere from the United Arab Emirates to New Zealand writing her $30,000 checks.

Here are four of Emily's best tips for successful campaigning.

1. **Answer the following four questions.** In any pitch, you have to be able to answer: *Why me? Why this? Why now? And why you?* Answer those four questions with as cleverly and well-told a story as possible and you'll have investors banging down the door. This applies to all kinds of crowdfunding. (See hack 37, Write the *Casablanca* of Decks.)

2. *Crowd* **comes before** *fund.* Too many crowdfunders mistakenly think that they'll build the audience while they raise the money. Invest time in building your crowd online before you ask them for funding, sharing great content and bringing them under the tent of what you're up to. Otherwise what you're attempting is a de facto friends and family push, which will limit your raise. How much lead time? "That depends on how much you're raising and how sticky your idea is," says

Emily. "But typically speaking, three to six months if you're going to raise in the $25,000 to $50,000 range in a very, very concerted effort."

3. **You can crowdfund more than once.** Don't make the mistake of thinking this is a "one and done" approach. You might crowdfund several times as your business approaches different milestones. Emily's first campaign raised $33,000. The second, which was the debt campaign, came a couple of years later and raised $500,000.

4. **Stand for something.** Something remarkable happened at Seed&Spark that demonstrates the power of knowing and sharing company values. Filmmakers work in an industry almost as notorious as technology for shutting out women and men of color, and Emily has always believed that crowdfunding could help them create new opportunities. After the 2016 presidential election, she decided to create #100Days ofDiversity, a campaign in which filmmakers on the platform made statements about how their project would increase diversity and inclusion in the industry, whether in front of the camera or behind it. Campaigns on Seed&Spark already had an amazing 75 percent success rate in achieving funding goals. Now, that rate shot up to 85 percent, and was holding steady at 80 percent—more than double their nearest competitor—when this book went to print.

She's clear on what's behind that boost: "We asked the filmmakers to stand for something—to think about what's important about their film beyond the film itself and to communicate that clearly to the audience. It was only going to be for one hundred days," says Emily, "but this is who we are now. So it's forever."

MICROHACK

Become a Crowdfunding Expert

Someone could write a book of hacks *just* on how to run a crowdfunding campaign. Fortunately, the major crowdfunding sites have created content to help you be successful—for example, IFundWomen.com has created a series of downloadables to coach you through every stage. Also spend time browsing campaigns that got fully funded—or, even better, any you have donated to. What was it that you watched, heard, and read that moved you to action?

Hack 36

Get the Traction You Need, Not the Traction They Want

CROWDFUNDING ISN'T MERELY a source of capital. It's a powerful way to show potential investors that you've got *traction*—which can be even more valuable than the dollars you raise from the campaign itself. A small amount raised from an enthusiastic crowd could help open the door to a much bigger round of funding.

So what is traction, exactly? Traction is quantifiable evidence that there's interest in and a market for your business. Winning a grant, receiving a loan, or being accepted into an accelerator are all early-stage forms of traction, as is the notorious "friends and family" round. But the most compelling traction (other than profitability) is *enthusiastic customers*—a growing number of people who are buying your product and telling others to do the same. Thus, crowdfunding is a genius leapfrog because you can rack up customers—and brand ambassadors, happily urging others to contribute—before you even have a product.

"If you have a business that's expensive to build but you have a bunch of customers champing at the bit to buy it once it's ready, well, that's something that you can take to investors that is irrefutable," says Emily Best. "Women and people of color will always be expected to have more traction than our mostly white, mostly male counterparts."

A successful crowdfunding campaign, then, is a traction tracker as much as a fundraising platform. The amount you raised, the number of donors, the number of hits your page got, the campaign's momentum—all these help an investor unfamiliar with your product or space to understand that the demand is there.

Traction should be as important to you as it is to investors. It's a way of checking your personal feelings about your business against cold data from the market. But if you're going to put your trust in metrics, they better be the right ones! Avoid the mistake of thinking that some investor, however deep-pocketed and successful, will be a better judge than you.

The terrific Christina Wallace, one of Mashable's "44 Female Founders Every Entrepreneur Should Know," has a textbook story to explain the danger of letting an outsider dictate your metrics. (Literally textbook: It was written up as a case study at Harvard Business School.) Christina's first startup, an online store that made custom-fit professional wear for women, crashed and burned eighteen months after its 2011 launch. She had built it with a friend a year after graduating from Harvard Business School (on scholarship; they do exist) and took funding from an investor who knew nothing about online retail. All he knew was that he wanted to invest in the internet and that the one-size-fits-all metric was growth in impressions—the number of people who visited their site.

Investor Man wrote impressions into Christina's term sheet (that's the agreement that sets the conditions for an investment) as a key performance metric; she had to grow that number to continue getting his money. So quite naturally, impressions became Christina's most important barometer, and her top goal was increasing traffic to the site. Meanwhile, she lost sight of something more critical in the long run: turning visitors into buyers, which is called *conversions* in sales jargon. There were other challenges with her business model, no doubt. But being hyperfocused on what was essentially a vanity metric cost her many opportunities to dig in and work on the real problems that needed solving. She satisfied her term sheet, but without creating enough meaningful revenue to move forward and garner more legitimate forms of traction.

So before you face the fundraising gauntlet, define traction for yourself so that you walk into every conversation with a strong, well-considered position on the metrics that matter and why. Assemble the data and create visuals that make it easy to see how you've grown that metric so far and where you can expect it to go in the near future.

Hack 37

Write the *Casablanca* of Decks

WHEN I SAY the *Casablanca* of decks, I don't mean that you need starkly beautiful photography or a tearjerker of a narrative. I mean you need to pay attention to the formula behind its storytelling. In pretty much every blockbuster Hollywood movie you can think of, two important things happen within the first ten minutes: The protagonist is introduced, and she experiences an "inciting incident" that interrupts the humdrum of her life and establishes a journey and, soon after, its stakes. (In those few movies that break the convention, most people start shifting in their seats, wondering whether they'll make it through two hours.) In the Golden Age cinema classic *Casablanca*, Rick (Humphrey Bogart) is entrusted with travel papers that will allow two people to escape the Nazi-controlled city. The stakes become clear when Rick's former lover shows up needing—you guessed it—travel documents to escape with her husband.

How does this apply to your deck? Think of your product as the protagonist and the financial ask as the incitement. I've sat in too many pitches when, ten slides in, the would-be founders still haven't revealed their product! They spend a small eternity establishing the problem and market size or relating the founder's origin story. I may be an atypical investor in some respects, but I'm exactly like most in one: I have no time. Hundreds of decks cross my desk, I have dozens of meetings every day, and I probably have a plane to catch on top of it. Aside from time constraints, data about market size (for example) easily floats into abstraction if it's not quickly met with the anchor of a solution.

But the deck sin that's a much bigger tell is a missing or buried financial ask. Recently I was pitched by an entrepreneur who buried the information about the size of her desired raise in a pile of bullets so deep, toward the end of the deck, that I wasn't even sure whether I was reading it correctly.

This needs to be bolded and in all caps: **FOUNDERS, DO NOT BURY YOUR FINANCIAL ASK.** You're looking for backers. This is why we're all here! This is the inciting incident! You need money to build your product to solve the problems! *Tell me the stakes!*

Buried financials is a frequent issue in decks I've vetted—particularly for women founders. It always leads me to three possible conclusions, none of them good. One, the founders are so afraid of money matters that I'm frankly concerned about their ability to run a company. Two, they doubt their own success and are therefore insecure about their ask. Or three, fundraising or not, they don't pay enough attention to the bottom line.

I want you to be confident enough in your ask to include not one but *two* slides detailing your raise. One early in the deck and one near the end.

Here are four more suggestions for mind-altering decks:

1. **Tell me why your team is uniquely qualified to build this business.** I recently heard a student pitch for wireless battery–charging hotspots. It seems like a great idea, but I was left with two questions: One, is this the technology that's finally going to finish off the world's honeybees? (Seriously, the global bee die-off keeps me up at night.) And two,

why you? I immediately thought that there must be thirty hardware companies with a substantial competitive edge over these two MBA students who merely had a neat idea, as far as I could tell from the pitch. Here, on the other hand, is a great example of a uniquely qualified founder: the amazing Dr. Lisa Dyson of Kiverdi. At the top of her field in physics and bioengineering, she and a colleague stumbled upon some old NASA research on carbon recycling in space and have now applied it to Earth to create food out of *carbon dioxide*. (Let that sink in: This could simultaneously feed people and fight global warming.) Kiverdi will bring those products to market. Lisa's background is so perfectly aligned to what she's doing that the entrepreneur and the business idea are pretty much inseparable.

2. **Answer "Why you?" for the investor as well.** Do the research so that you can call out explicitly why this investment firm is uniquely positioned to benefit from the investment and help bring the business to market. Yes, it takes more time up front, but the old-time sales chestnut "One hundred *no*s earn you one *yes*" is a waste of everyone's time in the long run. If you're getting one hundred *no*s, you're doing it wrong.

3. **Custom-tailor every deck you send.** Spamming potential employers with a generic résumé rarely results in success. It's the same with decks. This recently came up on a panel, when my co-panelist argued that any mission-driven company should declare that mission front and center as a core value. I know plenty of investors who would immediately write off such founders as fluffy and distracted from bottom-line concerns. Always lead with your values—when pitching to an audience that you know shares them. Otherwise they're a distraction, not an asset. So if you're solving a social problem, put that front and center in the deck for the impact investors. Pitching to a traditional investor who's more focused on

returns? Lead with the growth story. Know what your investors care about, and make sure your deck lines up.

4. **The deck doesn't make the business; the business makes the deck.** One impact-oriented VC told me that 80 percent of the companies that apply to her fund aren't ready for seed—and her assessment of "ready" is much broader than that of your typical VC. No deck can sell a business that's short on key fundamentals. Sometimes, in fact, the deck becomes the equivalent of looking at your own business through a magnifying glass; suddenly you see weaknesses that before you were able to squint away. Slow down and address these problems before seeking financing.

Amid all the anxiety about deck making, people forget that it's actually the easy part. The hard part is everything you've been working on in the other hacks: getting your financial house in order, attracting some initial outside capital, and building traction. If you've done all that, the deck is no big deal. You've got this.

MICROHACK

Use a High-Tech Spy Tool

Sending tailored decks is much easier with the help of an inexpensive service called DocSend. (I'm not shilling for them; I'm just a happy user.) DocSend tracks which deck goes to who, who's viewed it, and how long they spent on each page. This gives you important feedback about which sections are resonating with which groups, so you can improve your story over time.

Hack 38

Find Your Angels

I F YOU GOT the goods to build a great deck, you're ready to go after seed funding, otherwise known as *early-stage funding.* Two things get in women's way when it comes to seed. First, traditional seed investors are, like VCs, looking for companies they think could earn gargantuan returns—anywhere from ten times to forty times their investment. With that approach, they need to "win" on only a few of their bets to come out with strong returns.

As I've said, plenty of great companies—particularly outside of tech—don't fit that model. But even women with 10x-plus potential have been handicapped in fundraising by what VCs call *pattern recognition.* No matter how good the data, how ironclad the investment thesis, investors are still taking a leap of faith. Since they can't know the future, they look to the past for insight, searching consciously and unconsciously for patterns to help tell them what to do. The "pattern" of who makes it has been established by wunderkinder like Mark Zuckerberg—nerdy young white guys obsessively attached to keyboards. And this pattern, in turn, has almost certainly been informed by the "pattern" of the investors themselves: white men.

Thankfully for women, as well as for men of color, it's finally getting a little easier to find a seed investor who looks more like you. There's been a recent explosion in funds led by women and also by men of color, including Denmark West's Connectivity Capital, for example. The website speaks to their commitment to diversity: "We value a wide range of backgrounds, perspectives and approaches on our team and in our portfolio. We believe that this creates the capacity for greater empathy and opportunity."

Focusing on founders from underrepresented groups doesn't mean companies like Connectivity or Backstage aren't out to make money. "I'm a very sharky VC," says Arlan. "I'm looking at having obnoxious returns, too. But I can do pattern matching and see that a black woman in her forties can get these returns. A typical VC can't—he wants to see a hoodied white guy."

But an even better source for business capital is angel investors. Yes, there are other "micro-VC" seed options, for example Lattice Ventures or Comcast Ventures Catalyst Fund, which can be great flexible sources of early capital. But angels—accredited amateur investors—are unique in an important way: They're investing their own money and aren't beholden to anyone. They can do what they want. And because to be accredited (legally able to make equity investments) they need to make only $200,000 a year or have more than $1 million in assets, there's a very wide pool to choose from.

Legendary New York City angel Joanne Wilson, known on her blog as Gotham Gal, exemplifies why angels are such a strong match for women-owned businesses. Joanne has invested in more than 110 companies, in everything from luxury cannabis to stock discovery tools; about 65 percent have had women founders. She didn't start out with a plan to target women entrepreneurs, but when she started publishing her blog in 2004, women flocked to one of the few female faces in the field. And it didn't take long before she realized it was a smart investment thesis.

Here are a few reasons to find an angel like Joanne, based on an interview she gave on her podcast, *Positively Gotham Gal*:

Her "pattern" is very personal: "I invest in competitive survivors."

She's committed to more than return on her investment: "I like the journey more than anything else. . . . I'm not like, 'What's the exit here?'"

She's not rigidly held to 10x returns: "I at least want to make my money back."

She is a committed advisor to the companies she backs: "You can give advice, you can be helpful, you can be there, you can be a support, you can be a cheerleader, you can be a connector."

It used to be that angels, like VCs, were mostly men, but that's changing, too. Women's investment networks are springing to life around the country. Pipeline Angels is one. They hold boot camps around the country to train women angels and introduce them to women-led startups. More than three hundred Pipeline angels have now invested more than $5 million in more than fifty companies. Vicki Saunders's SheEO is another organization linking women with money to women founders who need it. She signs up "Activators" who contribute $1,100, which is then pooled and distributed to women-led businesses as low-interest loans that will be paid back and loaned out again to create a perpetual fund.

Here's my hack: Never forget that an angel can be . . . *anyone*. What I mean is that someone could start as your advisor and end up your angel, if both your business model and the relationship are strong. You only need to awaken them to the possibilities. For example, just before BRAVA launched, I invested in a company called TomboyX, which makes comfortable, non-frilly women's underwear. I started as their mentor at the women's startup accelerator MergeLane, and then I helped them find investors. In the process of getting to know the company well enough to pitch them, I got to know their numbers, and they sold me.

Is there an informal art to attracting the right advisors and then helping them get their wings? If there is, Chris Wilson is the master bell-ringer. I'm his friend but—of course—also became his angel; I'm an equity stakeholder in the book he sold to Putnam and in the movie he's working on now.

Chris has a crazy story you never forget. Warby Parker, as you might have seen, distills its company history into one hundred words that ship on a scrap of fabric with every pair of glasses. So here's Chris's Warby Parker story: Smart kid from DC who grew up with violence, hunger, and neglect. At seventeen, game over: He shot a man in self-defense and was sentenced to natural life in prison. Sixteen years later, in 2012, he got a second chance when he convinced a judge to reduce his sentence and let him leave. Five years after that, he had accomplished everything in the "master plan" to change his life that he wrote in his cell. He is finishing his college degree at the University of Baltimore, he started two businesses, and he works like a man on fire to create and find work for people from his new home, Baltimore—in particular, ex-offenders who need their second chance. (That's 118 words—not bad.)

Chris is making up for lost time, and he is 100 percent dedicated to giving more to the community than he takes. Maybe that makes it easier for him than for most people to turn strangers into angels. But that doesn't matter, because you need only a *fraction* of Chris's audacity and a fraction of his lift. Take his education at the University of Baltimore: After his first year, it was completely free. He enrolled paying tuition, but he realized that he needed to save money if he wanted to get his businesses off the ground. So he got a professor to put in a good word for him with the dean of the business school. Then he found the dean at a cycling class, told her his story. Told her how he's serving the community. Then he point-blank asked her to pick up his tuition, concluding, "I would be a good investment for you guys."

In Chris's words: "She just looked at me for a little bit and was like, 'Okay, well, if we were to find some money for you, you'd still need to pay for your school books.' I said, 'Dean, no disrespect. I don't want to pay for anything ever again.' It caught her off guard a little bit. She just looked at me and she said, 'What's your whole name?'"

Not only did Chris end up with a full ride, he has a stipend for living expenses and, in the dean, an angel for life. He's also received $25,000 to equip his first venture, an antique furniture restoration business; several thousand in bridge funds from his mentor to squeak by when he ran into a cash-flow crunch; and office space in Under Armour's Baltimore campus, as well as services from their design team. He never stops. So let's learn from Chris, and all the other Chrises out there, who, given the chance, would run circles around most of us. Unique as their circumstances may be, there are universal takeaways.

Get out there. A potential angel is more likely to be interested if they already know you or know of you. When Chris met Kevin Plank, the CEO of Under Armour (headquartered in Baltimore), Plank walked up to *him* and said, "Hey Chris, I'm Kevin." That's because Chris is everywhere. He's involved in community groups, activism groups, entrepreneurs' groups, and groups that are all three at once.

Get recommended. If he's dealing with someone who doesn't know him yet, Chris always, always asks someone else to establish his credibility, like he did with his professor and the dean at the University of Baltimore. When he met the dean, he had also just won a business competition, a fact that he didn't fail to mention.

Get a one-on-one meeting. Do whatever it takes to get face-to-face—whether it's a real meeting or, um, stalking the person at their cycling class. (Definitely a pro move, so proceed with caution.) But as Chris will tell you, "In the business world, at least in Baltimore, there's a lot of noise." You don't stand a chance when you're one of one hundred emails they got that day or some voice on a mobile.

Clarify your currency. Once you make it in the door, your job is to lay out clearly what they'll get out of advising you and your business—in Chris's case, it's always the measurable community impact his business success makes possible. Chris knows how to show people the receipts, a la hack 27. He keeps a count of how many people he's gotten jobs—252 when we last spoke, and, the real stunner, all but ten of those jobs paid more than minimum wage. But maybe even more important, Chris makes a point to always talk specifically about someone his work has recently helped. He makes sure his work is grounded in a real, human story, not just numbers.

Find your angels, and study them well. Because when I say an angel can be anyone, that means you, too. As soon as you have the wherewithal, put your money where it can have the most impact: in the hands of another smart woman entrepreneur.

MICROHACK

Write Your Warby Parker Story

Warby Parker tells its company story in one hundred words, starting with "Once upon a time." You should be able to do the same. Try it out on your own bio. It's not as easy as you'd think. Stick to three rules: You need a beginning, you need a middle, and you need an end. Now, the real hack: Where can you *put* your story so that it travels with your customer? Warby Parker puts it on a cleaning cloth and packs one with every pair of eyeglasses sold. Every single time a customer cleans her glasses, she's reminded of the story, and someone else might see it, too. And she's happy because she got a useful perk. How genius is that?

Hack 39

Be Mighty in the VC Power Play

CAROLINA HUARANCA, a principal at the venture firm Kapor Capital, told me that the fund receives thousands of pitch decks a year—and invests in fewer than twenty companies. That's the volume your typical VC is wading through. But here's what's unusual about Carolina and the Kapor team. Because Kapor is a social-impact fund committed to democratizing access to capital, they make sure *every* inquiry is read and *all* the passes get an explanation of why. So that means Carolina and her colleagues know more intimately than most that too many entrepreneurs are missing out on a giant opportunity to improve their fundraising outcomes.

"Often entrepreneurs send pitch decks without having done their homework—for example, to find out what sectors the fund invests in," says Carolina. "I weed out so many because they don't fit our investment thesis. The idea of intentionality is really important as you go through the fundraising process. For example, you're not likely to get our investment if we've already invested in a competitor. Yet I get several queries like that every day."

Don't send a query until you've done enough research to know whether you've got even a hint of a chance with a particular VC.

You won't even have to look far—you can find most of it on their website.

- Find their investment thesis: Does your company fit in with their vision? At Kapor, for example, it's all clearly laid out on a page called "Our Investment Criteria."
- Take a careful look at their existing portfolio: Does your company compete directly with any of their existing investments? (If yes, find out whether the fund makes competitive investments. Many don't.) Do you complement any?
- Find the specific partner who invests in companies like yours. For example, Carolina's bio clearly states that she invests in early-stage companies and is "particularly interested in Future Work, People Operations Technology, and Education."

Doing this research is super important for two reasons. For one, if entrepreneurs stop flooding VCs with blind queries, more of them might read their email rather than depending almost solely on warm leads, which is the state of affairs at most firms today. Or, at the very least, responsible investors like those at Kapor would spend less precious time writing generous "pass" letters.

The second reason to do your research is more direct in its impact on your success. The knowledge you amass about your potential capital partners and their field will make you mighty in the VC power play. And make no mistake, there is a power play. I've experienced it myself, pitching BRAVA's portfolio companies to other potential investors. Take a meeting I had with an early-stage investor who mostly had invested in tech but was looking to expand her portfolio. Not two minutes into our meeting I could tell she was one of those people who will eat you alive the moment they sense fear. I started pitching her on a pharma company, and when she heard the company didn't have revenue yet, she interrupted me to huff and puff: "What do you mean, no revenue?"

I didn't get defensive. I knew she was looking at the investment through the lens of tech, where investors often expect to see revenues and sales projections by Series A.

"This isn't tech; this is pharma. It's normal to have a Series A with no revenue because the company's still waiting on FDA approval," I said firmly.

Quick pause—then she nodded, said, "I get it," and we moved on. Because I had a ready response, her doubt turned into increased confidence and comfort that I just might be legit. If I had gotten defensive or stumbled, on the other hand, the meeting would have quickly careened downhill. She would have had all the power, and I would have had to scurry away like a mouse. I never let that happen, and neither can you. Keep your power by knowing their lens and yours. When there's a gap, be ready to meet their hesitation with a solid argument. It may not always resolve their concerns, but at least you leave the room feeling confident you presented well. And that feeling will make all the difference as you head into your next meeting.

If every VC meeting leaves you feeling like you walked in with little power and walked out with less, you're not going to survive your fundraising effort. So don't let that be the story. Walk in smart; walk out smarter.

Hack 40

Answer the $10 Million Question

ALL RIGHT ALREADY: Let's talk about exiting. I've disparaged exits here and elsewhere because I feel as though cashing out has become sensationalized in the story of entrepreneurship. But exits are a perfectly fine choice, even the right choice, for a certain kind of founder.

At what point does the possibility of an exit even become real? You start to be in the ballpark at around $10 million to $20 million in revenue, and $3 million to $4 million in profit. But your options at this point are determined by more than size, as Ivelisse Rodriguez, a partner at Avante Mezzanine Partners, told me when we talked about the kind of businesses she helps grow. She, like other investors, wants to see a sustainable business model, a diversified customer base, recurring revenue, a differentiated product or service, a great team, and a solid back office that can spit out accurate regular reporting.

Achieve all that, says Ivelisse, and you've entered a new universe. "A lot of women don't understand what kind of opportunities exist if you get to that level. You can get a partner who's smart and proven who will provide capital to do add-on acquisitions, bring in great people. . . . There are exceptional opportunities," says Ivelisse. "At my firm, we've built a network of hundreds of women in leadership positions who are looking to invest in women. If you get to $10 million in revenue, we'll help you get it to $100 million. There are women investors who want to help." And there's a ton of money out there, too. At the end of 2016, private equity firms had a whopping $820 billion available to invest in companies like yours.

So at that moment in the life of your business, it's time to ask yourself the $10 million question: *How should I grow?* Along with that you'll be asking the second question: *How should the company grow?*

You've got options, sister. Now could be the moment when a private equity firm comes in and buys a majority stake with plans to help you double, triple, or quadruple in size. If you think you'll love the challenges of a giant, complex organization, you'll want to stick around in some leadership role.

You might also find yourself missing those heady early startup days. I know plenty of founders-turned-CEOs who find themselves sitting on top of huge companies, going, "You know, I realize now that what I really love is starting a business, not running a mature one." Xochi Birch was one of those. She told me that if they had decided to raise money to grow Bebo bigger instead of selling it, she would have walked away. "I'm definitely a startup person. I love starting companies. When you're building a company, there can be a point when it outgrows you and it's not where you want to be anymore." If you've got the bug for serial entrepreneurship, exiting becomes your goal. You want to create a track record so that it becomes easier and easier to get investors to take you seriously, even at the idea stage.

But there's a third option: Stay small—relatively speaking, that is. Looking at most women-owned business today, you're already a whale. There's so much pressure to grow, grow, grow. Investors write off smallish companies as "lifestyle businesses," as if running a $5 or $10 million enterprise that provides gainful employment for twenty or fifty people means slacking off from "real business" in favor of tennis lessons and bonbons. They're wrong. More than 99 percent of U.S. companies have fewer than five hundred employees and account for about half of U.S. employees, according to the Small Business Administration.[1]

Just because they think it's a waste of their time, it's not a waste of your time—or of the people you employ or the customers you serve. Small businesses are the backbone of any healthy economy, and your impact doesn't need to be limited by how many zeros are on your yearly financial statement. If you ask me, we need more women-led businesses to grow into whales, and I have dedicated my life to ensuring that people like you have the tools and resources to do just that. But don't let anyone shame you into thinking that anything else is a failure. Anyone who turns up their nose at the small-to-medium-size business doesn't understand how economies thrive. You decide what success looks like, no one else.

SECTION 5

Grow

The growth of a business can sometimes feel like a series of crises. The reality is, it's hard to plan things so well that you avoid the "oh shit" moments. It's a learning process, for everyone.

I think about the designers Avani Patel works with at her incubator TrendSeeder. She helps save them when they finally get that first big order from Barneys and go, "Oh shit, how do I scale this fast?" That's a logistical crisis. They happen. You pick your way through them and manage through the chaos: increasing capacity, maintaining cash flow, adding employees, finding the right partners, and so on.

Solving these issues can create chaos and a sense of urgency—and while it may not feel like it, that's exactly the moment that you need to slow down, even halt, and reexamine your values. Because how you answer these tactical questions will ultimately determine whether you end up with a business that reflects your goals. Will you scale responsibly, with your core values guiding your decisions? Or will you chase down growth at any cost? I'm not judging either path, but I am urging you to choose yours consciously.

How Not to Choke on Growth

IT'S EASIER THAN you might think to lose yourself in the excitement of rapid growth. You can wake up one day and find you've become a monster or created one. I know that sounds dramatic, but I had that day, and I don't wish it on anyone. I was in my midtwenties. I had spent the past several years rising fast, no longer in startups but in massive tech companies. I had worked hard to blend in. (In truth, it came naturally to this lower-middle-class Latinx whose parents worked their immigrant butts off to install her in a wealthy, privileged world.) To compete with my male colleagues, I became the most aggressive. The most exacting. The hardest hard-ass in the room. I believed that if someone saw one soft spot, it would all be over. I'm competitive and like to win, and life had taught me that was the way to do it. I was rewarded for my behavior again and again.

And so I became the boss. At twenty-six, I parachuted (not literally, but it felt that way) into Dublin to solve a massive implementation problem with our biggest client, the most famous technology company in the world at that time. Several others had been sent in and failed. I decided that the only way to move forward was to assemble our remote team into one space. I yanked every member of the project team from four different countries, flew them to Dublin, and put them to work. For four months, we worked days, nights, and weekends. The schedule was tight, and millions of dollars and my reputation were on the line. So of course I had everyone working insane hours with no breaks.

The day of our deadline, I walked into the office with a big smile on my face: We were ready to port in the data, the final step of our delivery. All that needed to happen was for a guy named Stephen to carry out the complex chain of logins, passwords, and process steps that were needed to initiate the transfer of files. Have you guessed where this is going? Minutes after I arrived, one of my team members meekly delivered some news: Stephen had called in sick that morning.

After cursing myself for allowing our victory to be dependent on a single employee (the real root issue here), I made a snap decision. By that point, everyone was so afraid of me that when I said, "Jump," people said, "How high?" So no one dared to question me when I ordered my driver and two team members to go to Stephen's home, bring him in, and not let him leave until he had trained two employees to ensure we'd never be stuck like that again. So it went. Stephen got in the car and did the training, and we started dumping data. From my point of view, the day ended better than it had begun. We were delivering on time, a catastrophe was averted, and I spent that night the same way I had spent many, many nights, entertaining our upset clients until 4:00 a.m. I probably stayed out even later than usual, sure that this would be among the last of such evenings, with our success so close at hand.

The next day, I hadn't been in the office more than two minutes when the same employee walked up.

"Stephen called in sick—" she told me.

I cut her off, smug as could be.

"I don't effing care anymore. I've trained two other people."

She stood up taller and cleared her throat, no longer meek.

"If you had let me finish, I was going to say this: He called in sick. This time from the hospital's cardiac care unit."

Whomp. Stephen was a little bit more than sick.

In that moment, reality hit—hard. I had nearly worked someone to death, it seemed. (He did recover.) It took me years to unpack what that meant to me. How to address it, whether and how to atone. Today I can see clearly that I put so much attention on how to blend, how to be successful on *others'* terms, that I forgot to consider and set my own. I may have been born to strive and compelled to lead—but I was also raised with a credo of kindness and care that I had strayed far, far away from.

In the years since, I've plotted every decision I've made regarding my career, my business, and my relationships with certain values in mind. I'm not perfect, but I am very clear on the blueprint. And today I can tell you, through the proof of my own experience, that you *can* succeed and thrive by being human and by caring for others. I'm still blunt AF, but that's what *outcomes, not optics*, demand. And I'm direct, not ruthless.

One of my first tasks for BRAVA was to sit in a room with someone I trusted—the branding expert Aviva Mohilner—to spend an entire day charting the values that we'd live and breathe by. Aviva has found that values are the missing element when entrepreneurs sit down to name their company or shape their brand. Not only did I mark time for this work, I marked space for it: I did it while I was on vacation in Ecuador, a place that helps me return to my gentlest, most grounded self—the self that can at times get worn down by an unrelenting schedule and the daily grind of startup life.

To apply Aviva's basic process to your own business, start with a brainstorm to generate the five words that best reflect your vision. If you have a team, they're your natural partners in this. If you're still a one-woman show, pull in someone who knows you and the business well. Once you have five words, use them to develop a clear statement of your guiding principles. In BRAVA's case, we had:

1. **Big Thinking:** When it comes to scale, returns, or impact, we don't play small.
2. **Triple-Committed:** We are unwavering in our dedication to the companies we invest in, our investors, and the economic well-being of women.
3. **Principled Leadership:** We take a stand and are willing to make unpopular decisions in service to what we believe.
4. **Resourceful Advisors:** We put our knowledge, experience, and extensive network to use for our portfolio companies.
5. **Supporting Disruption:** We invest in innovative business models in high-growth industries that substantively affect women's lives.

There's another reason why the moment you start to grow is the moment to get clear and explicit about exactly what you are committed to. As a microenterprise, it was just you. The impact you had was limited in scope. But as your business grows, your team will, too. Your operating principles will be theirs. If you empower people, they'll thrive and pay it forward. If you're a monster, they'll mirror that. You'll be setting the tone and MO for a culture that will ultimately pervade the rest of the organization, no matter how big you grow. And not only is that problematic from a human point of view, it's also why many companies sometimes hit a wall. (Uber, anyone?) It's more than how people are treated in the workplace. What happens inside the walls of your company leaks out into your product, your marketing. Nothing truly great can be built and sustained over time by a culture that sucks. The shortcut: Get it right *now*, while it's just you or a few employees. If it seems hard with a few, imagine doing it with a thousand.

Hack 42

Build a Movement, Then a Market

THERE'S YET ANOTHER reason to be clear on the values you stand for before you attempt to grow. It becomes your marketing campaign. Actually, let's not even call it that. Your real focus shouldn't be growing a market. It should be building a movement.

If you had told me ten years ago that I'd someday get up at 7:00 a.m. and sweaty-dance with five hundred people on a boat off Manhattan, I would have laughed. If you had then told me I would do all that with a smoothie instead of a cocktail in my hand, I would have laughed so hard I cried. What?! But I have done exactly that, and so have thousands of people around the world, at an event called Daybreaker, all because Matthew Brimer and Radha Agrawal sat down one late night at a Williamsburg falafel shop and decided to create a movement.

The word Matthew uses most to talk about all this is *community*. From the get-go, he believed that the Daybreaker community would be as valuable to the people it attracted as the "product" itself. He had founded his first business, the tech academy General Assembly, on that premise and watched it catch fire. Now, he and Radha wanted to build a community based on five core values: self-expression, wellness, camaraderie, mindfulness, and mischief.

(This last is my favorite. Mischief, per Matthew, is breaking the rules with love. That's exactly what leapfrogs are!) Unlike Burning Man, their tribe would all be interested in exploring radical free expression completely sober.

With values as their guide, the idea they hatched neatly filled a gaping hole in New York's social scene. Going out in this city is like being a contestant on *The Bachelor*: It's a meat market, and the producers are constantly trying to get you drunk. Finding a truly safe space to let loose in your average dance club? Good luck with that. Besides which, in New York City, you've got a lot of ambitious kids who want to party midweek but also care about showing up at work at 9:00 a.m. rested and ready to produce. Staying out until 4:00 a.m. doesn't fit their lifestyles.

Matthew sums it up: "Normally people don't wake up early in the morning and dance their face off, but if that is how we want to live, and if that inspires and connects people and makes them feel amazing and creates community and does good things for the world, then great, let's do that." They figured worst-case scenario, "Nobody shows, and we woke up too early one day."

Four years later, they're in more than twenty cities around the world and have a clothing line, a content channel, a burgeoning Daybreaker college program, and a plan to add a bunch of new cities. Since their very first event, everything they've done—every product decision, business partnership, expansion, and hire, every email, every status update—is oriented around those five original values.

In the years since Daybreaker popped up, I've noticed a parallel trend of people flirting with total sobriety, finding healthy alternatives to "juice" their social lives. I see Facebook and blog announcements about people doing dry months, even dry years. It's become a thing, at least in techie circles in New York, San Francisco, and LA. Natalia Oberti Noguera of Pipeline Angels announced on Instagram that they're only hosting alcohol-free gatherings going forward, as part of their commitment to creating safe spaces. I bet others will follow.

I absolutely believe that Daybreaker has played a role in helping encourage this trend. Matthew, the smarty-pants, is a bit more cautious. "I like to believe that Daybreaker is both a cause and an effect. We didn't start the wellness movement, certainly, but I think we supported it, and we also benefited from it." Matthew also points out that Daybreaker gives people a new experience to draw from. "It proves to people you can have an epic, ridiculous fun time and feel great socially, physically, and emotionally all without the need for alcohol as a crutch," he says. "Proving that to the public I think is a big step."

So how do you build the kind of movement that spreads through the world like a pro-social virus? The answer will be unique to each company. But if you want to learn from one formula that worked, Matthew's is a good one.

- **Establish your values up front.** Great! If you've followed through on the last hack, you've already done that.
- **Seed the community.** Light the spark. For Daybreaker, Matthew and co. handpicked three hundred friends who they knew personally shared their five values and would immediately "get" it. Choose your early customers strategically: Three hundred people who you have strong reason to believe will love what you do and what you stand for will create a lot more spark (read: growth from word-of-mouth) than three thousand people who go, "Meh."
- **Make them insiders.** People lucky enough to be on the first guest lists were encouraged to share the invite with deserving friends but asked not to post publicly on social media. The event page was password-protected. Like a club with a secret knock, the event took on an air of underground cool. "I've done a number of events in my day and especially when

something is early, before it's proven and has credibility as being a thing that everyone knows is awesome, you have to find other things to make it attractive. Something that is underground, kind of secret, that not many people know about it and isn't for everyone is a good way to get people excited," says Matt. The universal point here is that when people love you, find ways to love them back. Make them feel privileged to be a part of what you're doing.

- **Make it a good story.** Daybreaker never put a single dollar toward PR. Reporters came to them. For about two years, they had a positive press hit every week. Why? "[The media] just couldn't really believe it," Matt says. "They were like, 'Wait a minute, all these people like waking up and going to dance in this crazy, colorful, performance-driven party at seven a.m. and there's no alcohol and then they go to work?' It was just mind-blowing."

- **Create spaces for the community to gather.** For Daybreaker, this was seamless. The product itself was the gathering. If you're selling a widget or a fancy hat, you're going to have to work a little harder. You might host events or create really lively social media channels. The time you spend helping your customers meet is worth it: Most businesses see themselves as the hub and their customers as spokes, each in their own aisle. Movement-oriented businesses help their customers cross out of their lonely little aisles to build a web. That's the key to impact. Says Matt, "When someone smiles on the dance floor at Daybreaker at another attendee and they smile back and do a little dance move together, that didn't cost us anything. But both of those two customers leave a little bit happier."

Bottom line, you don't start a movement by thinking about your customers as isolated targets. Community building starts on day 1.

Hack 43

If You Want Friends, Create Controversy

YOU DON'T GET the spotlight by being meek and wishy-washy. As I said in hack 35, you've got to stand for something. Now let's add a level: Get comfortable with pissing people off. This is another arena where leapfroggers or any newcomers to business have a serious leg up over corporations. Corporations are terrified of pissing people off. They're famous for issuing careful non-statements that say nothing in hopes of alienating nobody. You, on the other hand, have little to lose by declaring your beliefs. But first you need the courage to make enemies. And the unflappable dignity to rise above their trolling.

Taking a stand isn't enough to attract interest. Controversy—and with it, publicity—follows when you find an honest way to surprise people and/or royally piss them off.

Katharine Zaleski, the cofounder and president of PowerToFly, found a way to do both. PowerToFly is the platform that connects millions of women to enterprises that are committed to building more diverse and inclusive environments. Dell, American Express, and Goldman Sachs are a few of their partners. (I'm a strategic advisor there and was the chief revenue officer in their early days.) When Katharine and her cofounder, Milena Berry, wanted to get their story out, Katharine didn't write an op-ed rehashing the dire circumstances for mothers in the modern workforce. Yawn. That story has been told a million times, and apparently no one cares because the majority of workplaces still penalize mothers.

Instead, Katharine published a personal essay on Fortune.com with a provocative take: "For mothers in the workplace, it's death by a thousand cuts—and sometimes it's other women holding the knives." The piece ran with the headline "I'm Sorry to All the Mothers I Worked With" and led with Katharine sharing that she had never followed up on a partnership deal when the potential partner was a proud mother with "endless photos of her small children spread across the airy space. . . . She wasn't the first and only mother whose work ethic I silently slandered."[1]

Are you feeling worked up? Katharine went on to explain how becoming a mother herself had not only opened her eyes to her bad behavior but led her to leave her job to start PowerToFly. By admitting that she had been silently complicit in the stereotyping and mistreatment of mothers, Katharine had added a new spin to an old story. Her raw honesty ripped open the floodgates of controversy. Not everyone liked what she had to say, but *everyone* had a reaction.

The article quickly went viral. Soon the story was on CNN and in the *Daily Mail, Business Insider, BuzzFeed . . .* pretty much everywhere. Within twenty-four hours, Katharine was doing her makeup for the *Today* show. Her confessional essay (possibly the internet's most popular literary art form) had created the perfect vehicle to ignite a conversation about how to support working moms. Quite the opportune moment to introduce a useful new platform: PowerToFly, a marketplace to match companies with women techies in search of remote work, where productivity rather than face time becomes the operative measure of a worker's contribution. Three months later, they had raised $6.5 million in fundraising commitments and landed major corporate clients such as *The New York Times*.

Controversy can provide the platform to introduce you, your business, and your message to the world. Gloria Feldt, one of my feminist heroes and the former CEO of Planned Parenthood, included it among the nine tools she's identified to help women step into our power. She urges women to see it as a way to make people think, to make yourself a teacher, and to clarify your own values and others. (More on this in her outstanding book, *No Excuses: Nine Ways Women Can Change How We Think About Power*.)

I'm convinced Katharine's story moved so far, so fast not just because it was provocative but because it was *personal*. You've probably watched a few TED Talks—for example, Brené Brown's lecture on vulnerability (more than thirty-two million views and counting) or Susan Cain's on the strength of introverts (eighteen million and counting). There's a reason why TED Talks have become synonymous with viral, sticky content—stories people want to share. They cracked the code. The now familiar format of the five-to-fifteen-minute lectures is to start with a moving personal story and then shift to a universal insight, generally backed with some exciting research or inquiry.

I'm not going to teach you how to tell an arresting personal story in one hack. As you now know, I went to theater school and only barely scratched the surface. I highly recommend you spend some time immersing yourself in that world, whether as a student or merely as a spectator.

What I *can* tell you is where to look for help. There's an entire industry of coaches for public speaking and pitching—but I don't hire those people, not for myself and not to train the young entrepreneurs at my summer camp. I hire artists.

The challenge is that they often don't think they know anything about narrative in a nonfiction setting, especially a business setting. The benefit of hiring a business-oriented speaking coach is that they're well versed in both sides of the coin. So to work with an artist instead, you need to learn how to lead them into it. The secret is to build in constraints. You say, "I'm going to tell you the forty-five-minute story of me and my business. I'm going to tell you who my audience is. Then you're going to give me the most compelling thirty-second or two-and-a-half-minute story for that audience. Help me throw out everything that's extraneous or boring, and whittle it down to just that gripping angle that's going to get people listening. Then help me learn to communicate it."

If you're thinking, "Oh, I got this—I'm a great speaker, and I don't need help," let me tell you: I thought that about myself until last year. I arrived at an event where I was scheduled to give a speech about negotiation. I looked at the agenda and saw that they had scheduled me to follow Supreme Court Justice Sonia Sotomayor. Give me a break! I took another look at my boring negotiation lecture and mentally ripped it up. Fortunately, my friend Andy is a former theater director and producer. The honest truth is that Andy not only is better at telling a story than I am, he also could see *me* with a perspective that I don't—can't—have, no matter how self-aware I think I am. And he isn't the kind of person who thinks my shit smells like roses. And so he took my ideas and hacked and whittled: "Nope, not this. Cut this. Change that." Fast and furious, we rewrote the entire speech in a few hours, and the result was *one thousand times better* than where I started. Not only was it more personal and more honest, it was also more provocative. (You can judge it yourself on YouTube at bit.ly/gettono. You'll recognize the subject matter from hack 4, on getting to *no*.)

When I line up speakers for Barnard's TEDx events, I do the same thing—I pair everyone with a theater professional as a coach. I actually coached real estate mogul and *Shark Tank* star Barbara Corcoran personally, after she initially balked at needing it. Yes, she is a polished TV presence, but delivering a TED Talk onstage is another animal.

The truth is, trying to learn on your own how to be a master storyteller is like jumping into a rabbit hole—you may never find your way back out. PR reps are amazing at finding a provocative angle, no doubt. But there's nothing like a professional storyteller to prepare you to bring your voice into the world, loud enough and honest enough to make an impact.

I've repeated the word *honesty* a number of times in this hack, for a couple of reasons. First, any story with a whiff of pretension or falsehood is likely to fall flat. People smell it right away, particularly when it's explicitly or implicitly connected to the personal interest of your business. But second, being 100 percent authentic to who you are protects you when the trolls inevitably emerge. They can get mad, spit, and scream all they want. It's a lot easier not to care, and for others not to care, when you know that whatever happens, you've spoken your truth.

MICROHACK

Shout-Out the Trolls

Getting attacked by trolls? Try out iheartmob.com, a platform that gives real-time support to anyone dealing with online harassment. Or build your own heart mob by asking others in your community to rally behind you. We did that for Kimberly Bryant and Black Girls Code, after Kimberly turned down a $125,000 grant from Uber—a shallow gesture, given that they had just promised nearly ten times that amount to Girls Who Code. After one weekend of campaigning on Twitter, we had raised $145,000. The story caught the attention of executives at Lyft, who later invited Black Girls Code to partner in its Round Up & Donate program, making it easy for Lyft riders to donate to the nonprofit. While I'd like to rid the world of trolls, they at least can fire up the people who care about you.

Read the Media's Mind

Hᴇʀᴇ's ʜᴏᴡ ᴛᴏ successfully pitch a journalist: Solve their problem. Give them a story idea that they can plug and play. Communication strategist Rakia Reynolds of Skai Blue Media told me how the pros make this happen so that leapfroggers can join in.

You probably already know that every magazine, digital or print, works around a preplanned editorial calendar. An editor in February knows exactly what kind of stories she needs to put in motion for May, or sometimes even for February of the following year.

Here's the insider's 411: These calendars are *available to the public.* Right now, you can go to a magazine's website—or sometimes its parent company's site—and search for the *media kit,* which will include the calendar. If the kit's not on the site, there's almost always an email listed to request it. There: You've cracked the Rosetta stone. Now you know what an editor is looking for, six to nine months out. Meaning that for most print glossies, you need to be pitching six to nine months in advance.

But wait, there's more! A shortcut within the shortcut. As you start requesting calendars, you'll start to notice a lot of synergy—editors working on similar topics, according to Rakia, or with a large degree of overlap. There's a reason for that. These editors are all leaning on a tool to generate their own calendars called *Chase's Calendar of Events* (bit.ly/chasecal), and you can go right now and buy it online for less than $100—still spendy, but a solid investment. (And maybe your mastermind group shares the cost with you . . . ?)

Rakia says, "I've been using *Chase's Calendar of Events* for years, because after evaluating so many different editorial calendars, I've seen that this is what matches up. Every month has specific themes that journalists use to build out their story planning, everything from National Small Business Week to Global Accessibility Awareness Day."

Here's the sticky but not unsolvable challenge: You don't have a relationship with these people the way a PR pro does. To be taken seriously, you need to do the legwork to establish a distinct and authoritative voice. You need credibility builders and an editorial calendar of your own. Once you have the message, social media is the medium.

Ashley Graham is a fun example from Rakia's roster. She's a supermodel whose high-profile press hits started piling up after Rakia and her team advised her. They worked with her to develop a TED Talk called "Plus-Size? More Like My Size" (http://bit.ly/plussize mysize), which she delivered at TEDxBerkleeValencia in 2015. This talk was the anchor of a social media campaign that positioned Ashley as an icon and role model for body-positive self-empowerment. As her following and exposure grew, so did her career, leading to her history-making appearances as the first plus-size model to grace major magazine covers. Now Graham, less than three years since that TED Talk, is much more than a supermodel. She's a mogul with a book, a lingerie line, and much more in the works.

The takeaway, says Rakia: "Build your own authoritative voice. Establish what that voice is going to be in the market, make an editorial content plan for social media, and stick to it." While you may push this voice out through your business's social handles, it's a lot easier to be authentic and engaging—not to mention mediagenic—if you're speaking as an individual, not behind an anonymous business identity.

To figure out what topics you'll cover, ask yourself three questions:

1. What problems does my business solve?
2. What do my customers care about?
3. What do I stand for? (You've answered this already if you worked through hack 41, How Not to Choke on Growth.)

Once you know your topic area, pull out your little folder of editorial calendars and *Chase's Calendar* and look for synergies—places where you can align to what everyone else is going to be doing. And finally, don't make the mistake Rakia sees all the time, which is taking a "one and done" approach to long-form content.

Say you get an article placed somewhere or are interviewed. Most people post the link to all their social feeds and then forget about it, detouring to random topics in social or going silent. A smart leapfrogger uses that one article to fuel six months of social content.

"Maybe your article was six hundred to eight hundred words. You probably had fifteen different pieces of shareable content there," says Rakia. Using your gut and those editorial calendars, pick six directions, and use them to build out six months of content. "Dissect it so that at the top of every single month, you're using that one quote, or those one or two sentences, to be your theme for the month, then build content out around that."

Once you've got your content engine churning, any editor can click through the links you'll include in your pitch email and see that you not only know what you're talking about, you've got people listening. In the days before you can afford to get a PR person to vouch for you among the press, social proof and smart content are your go-to work-arounds.

Hack 45

Out-Kardashian the Kardashians: The New Influencer Marketing

DUMB INFLUENCER MARKETING: Get your product in the hands of a celebrity who has a little influence over a million followers. Smart influencer marketing: Get your product in the hands of a niche expert who has a lot of influence over a thousand followers. Or even better, become the influencer yourself.

Smart influencer marketing is the perfect tool for leapfroggers. You don't have the bucks or the access to hire LeBron James or Kim Kardashian West. Who cares anymore? The odds are that a celebrity delivers more on optics than impact, which as you know by now is not our way.

How do I know this for sure? Because cutting-edge social media companies have the data that proves it. I recently chatted up Gil Eyal, the cofounder of one of those companies. His company HYPR is hired by global brands to help them do smarter influencer marketing on a massive scale, by providing in-depth audience analytics for more than ten million influencers. Talking to Gil, I started to realize that the driving insights behind HYPR's offering teach essential lessons for leapfroggers.

Big brands, says Gil, are guilty of dumb influencer marketing all the time. Here's a great example: Kate Upton used to be the face of Bobbi Brown. She looks good in the makeup, and she has millions of followers, but can she get women to spring for a new lipstick? HYPR knows the answer: Not through social media she won't. The platform tracks one billion social accounts twice a week to see which accounts actually influence others. "If you look at Kate Upton, she has an enormous audience, but it's almost entirely men hoping she'll post bikini pictures. About 30 percent of her audience visits a porn site the same day that they visit her social posting. How much makeup is she really selling?" says Gil. "Could this brand, or really any other makeup brand, do much better by finding lesser-known people on YouTube who have a very female audience who have followed them specifically to learn about makeup tips?"

The answer is yes, and getting that YouTube expert to rep your makeup would probably cost a fraction of what Bobbi paid Kate Upton. Big brands absolutely need HYPR's service; you can do it yourself, for now. In the world of self-made social influencers, big brands are outsiders. You're not—or if you are, you can change that. Leapfroggers can create their own access and brand allies by becoming experts themselves, entrenching themselves in the space.

Lisa Leonard is a perfect example. She's a California mom who makes jewelry for moms—handcrafted pieces "that can be worn with jeans or your little black dress." The jewelry is hand-stamped with kids' names, dates, and other meaningful phrases. (As one fan told me, "It's a reminder on the darker days of parenting that what sometimes feels like servitude is really quite magical.") Lisa started her business fifteen-odd years ago when her first son was born so that she could work at home. Now she has more than twenty employees, multiple store locations, and a web of artisans in California and Israel who produce her handcrafted jewelry at a scale she almost certainly never imagined in the early days. She and her husband—who, by the way, has a dad blog, a lonely corridor—have also now launched a line of leather bags, Leonard Lane.

Lisa was propelled from microbusiness to multimillion-dollar brand in large part by smart influencer marketing. Moms didn't hear about her jewelry because she got Jessica Alba to wear it or because it was featured on TV or in a glossy magazine. They heard about it because their favorite mom bloggers wear it or hosted ads for it. These are bloggers most people never heard of but who have dedicated, die-hard followings of a thousand readers or more. Lisa put herself at the epicenter of that network by becoming a blogger herself, writing about topics like the birth of her children, the challenges and gifts of parenting a disabled son, the stuff she likes, and more. Lisa *is* her customer, and she has been hyperstrategic in communicating that to build her empire.

So how do you emerge from the shadows and build your own niche as a microinfluencer? Start being vocal on social media about what you know. Over time you'll build an audience and community who understands they'll be educated or entertained (hopefully both!) by listening to you. The metric to focus on isn't how many followers you have but how much impact you have on them. Do they comment back? Do they share your posts? Do they rave about your business? And most important, do they click Buy Now?

You also should put more focus on building actual relationships with a small circle of bloggers in your space than on upping your Instagram or Facebook follower count. "You could be a small brand and have a thousand of your own followers, but partner with fifteen or twenty other people who have five thousand followers," says Gil. "That way you're going to have a much bigger impact. The strength of the relationship is much stronger, and you're not wasting energy on people who could not care less."

When it comes to growing your influence on social media, here are my top four tips:

1. Throw out the vanity metrics such as "likes" and follower counts, and focus on shares and real-time exchanges.
2. Participate in others' conversations until you have the authority to start your own.
3. Don't ever pretend you're something you're not.
4. Define what's valuable to people, and then make sure that 80 percent of your posts deliver it. (Reserve the other 20 percent for artful nonsense and cute animal pics, which never get old.)

Hack 46

Hire Smart and Tap a New "Monster"

W HEN IT'S TIME to hire up, don't do it yourself. Just don't. Hiring is the most difficult task business owners face and one of the worst places we can screw up. A bad hire can gut punch your entire business, particularly when you're small.

But beyond that, there's a risk in relying on your own networks or traditional channels to make hires. It's an easy mistake to make: The candidate whose résumé comes in referred by someone you trust feels like a sure thing. But here's the problem: Referrals limit your search to your existing network or one step beyond. In most cases, that approach assures that the candidates you get are going to look and think like you: same ethnicity, same socioeconomic background, same schools, same clubs.

You, intrepid woman entrepreneur, are building a business that matters. You're better than that. You want, you *need*, to get your opportunity in front of a diverse pool of applicants. I know you do. You might think that you'll get there by casting your net wider—say with a Monster or LinkedIn search—and being intentional in your language, color-blind in your vetting process, etc., etc. Don't count on it. If your business has grown beyond a handful of employees and you're serious about recruiting women and talented individuals who slip through the traditional "wide net," my best hack is to use one of the recruitment companies specialized to solve this problem. Their raison d'être is to find those candidates, vet them, and match them with interested companies where their work will make a difference. They're the experts. PowerToFly offers subscription access to their database of women tech workers, as well as matching services. (They focus on matching remote workers with large businesses, so if you're hiring your first team members, they're not for you.) Jopwell focuses on people of color. A company called Catalyte uses artificial intelligence to identify individuals, regardless of background, who have the innate potential and cognitive ability to be great software developers. (You have to be a pretty big player to hire Catalyte, but hopefully that won't always be the case.) These are a few resources I know and trust, but there are other companies out there, and new ones launching all the time, that are dedicated to serving this need.

If you're too small to hire a recruitment firm, here are three things you can do to improve your chances of creating a team that's both talented and diverse:

1. Make sure that everyone involved in vetting candidates is assessing them against a clear checklist of skills and experiential requirements for success in the role. No one should be giving anyone a thumbs-up based on instinct or their shiny personality.
2. Don't make hiring decisions based only on direct referrals from your network. Share job postings with connectors and resources that you know will reach beyond your personal bubble, whatever shapes it.
3. For help fighting gender bias, check out Iris Bohnet's book, *What Works: Gender Equality by Design*, which offers tips to ensure women aren't turned off by your job ads. For example, keep the list of required qualifications limited to the must-

haves, not the nice-to-haves. Women are less likely than men to apply to jobs for which they don't meet every listed requirement.

Here's the second half of my hiring hack: Don't be afraid of remote workers. Think carefully about whether a job requires someone local. I have had a number of assistants over the years, as my needs changed with different phases of life and business. But it was PowerToFly that really got me thinking about whether I needed someone in one of my hubs. My main base is New York, but 95 percent of what I need an assistant to do could happen anywhere with stable Wi-Fi, so long as the assistant was willing to keep up with my time zones.

I hired an assistant from North Carolina. She was an African American LGBT woman in a state that's increasingly toxic to gay folks, and she was happy to have an employer from somewhere else. I learned from her PowerToFly profile that she was a leader in her local LGBT community. She didn't want to leave, but she needed a professional challenge. Meanwhile, I needed an enthusiastic, smart, impeccably qualified assistant. Done! Later my team grew, and hiring someone nearby became more important, but at the time, she was my perfect match.

Having a diverse team isn't just about doing good. Women are half the population but control much more than half the buying power. Meanwhile, the country is turning brown. What some people call "minorities" will be the majority by 2060, according to our friends at the U.S. Census Bureau.[1] Already, 50.2 percent of the twenty million children under five years old in the U.S. are kids of color. Building a business whose team looks nothing like its customers isn't just asinine; it's bad for business.

MICROHACK

Find Your Muse

Hiring top talent is harder than you'd think. The competition in many industries is so stiff that a great salary and free candy 24–7 no longer seal the deal. Prospective employees want to know what kind of tribe they'll be joining—and they want to hear about it from employees themselves. A business I like called The Muse has stepped in to offer applicants a better window into the companies (and the people) behind each job posting. The Muse is an upgrade from LinkedIn or Monster because, if you put in the time to create a profile there, what you get is much better than the huge pile of résumés that tend to come in from a typical job posting. Instead, you can expect a small selection of qualified candidates, which is a time saver and a lifesaver if it means you find people who really "get" your business.

Grow Fast by Joining Forces

So you've sweat the sweat and put in the hours and built your company to a certain size—say, $500,000 in annual revenue. Congrats! That's a serious business you've got. And yet. . . . What could you be doing with double the revenue? Maybe you could operate at greater efficiency or finally afford to take on that next employee who could then help you grow even bigger. But how to make that jump, when capital is scarce? It eludes many leapfroggers, remaining a permanent *what if?*

But what if you could make it happen overnight?

My friend Monika Mantilla opened my eyes to the hack that can do it. Monika is a private investor whose firm Small Business Community Capital (SBCC) is an SBIC Impact fund. The SBIC is an SBA program that matches private investors with low-interest leverage. But as with many programs, Monika has a size requirement: She can only invest in companies with $1 million EBITDA and above. (EBITDA stands for Earnings Before Interest, Taxes, Depreciation, and Amortization, and it's used to measure the performance of companies.)

When Monika sees an awesome founder with a strong company, spitting out cash with incredible growth potential but still beneath that threshold, she doesn't say "Rats," and walk away. She starts sniffing around for another company that would make a natural partner and also be served by growing. Then she introduces the two and helps them merge. Overnight, they're a new entity with EBITDA over $1 million. And voilà, they are now eligible for investment.

Before talking to Monika, I hadn't really thought about mergers as a leapfrog to help take businesses over that critical hump from microenterprise to small business, or small business to mid-market (which means revenue of $10 million and up). When I hear "M&A," I think of my own experience working within a multinational; we were more in the business of hostile takeovers than win-win partnerships. Mergers and acquisitions (M&A) are how giant corporate entities gobble up new territory and eliminate competition. But there's no reason that small companies can't improve their lot by pursuing true partnerships, mergers, or even acquisitions—a bigger company absorbing a smaller one—that produce wins for everybody.

Why don't more small businesses think in this way? My guess is because we're working so hard to squeak out that next $10,000 or $100,000 of revenue that we forget to look for the shortcut—the smart move that would make 1 + 1 = 3. Also, our sense of what's possible is shaped by our experience, up until the point that we're lucky enough to meet a Monika. (Or smart enough to have read all the way to hack 47. *Brava!*)

So how do you identify that perfect partner? Just like big companies, you're looking for synergies—those aspects of your partnership that will create value so that 1 + 1 = 3. Here are four possible synergies to explore:

1. Are your offerings complementary enough to cross-sell, expanding business with current customers? For example, a corporate diversity training consultancy might partner with a recruiting firm that could help them deliver new talent.

2. Does the alliance expose each of you to new markets or channels of business? For example, imagine an exercise studio joining forces with a company offering on-demand private training. Now the gym has a new service to attract higher-end clientele, and the private trainers have access to a steady, built-in customer base.

3. Can you merge your staff to create greater efficiency? This one requires you to be ready to potentially let some of your existing team go.

4. Can you reduce waste and churn by sharing rent, equipment, and other costs?

Remember, it's easy to get cozy inside the boundaries of what you've already created. So if you're really serious about growing, force yourself to dedicate time to looking outside your business for more than just ideas. Look for opportunities to join forces and supercharge that growth.

Hack 48

Find Partners Who Make Any New Market "Local"

IF YOU'RE MOVING into unknown turf, you need partners who know your new customers. So many companies—mostly giant corporations but also some hubris-ridden tech companies—stumble when they try to expand. I remember the challenge of translating the game Cranium into British English, one of my earliest projects. It wasn't really a translation so much as a total rewrite—what Brits would enjoy and find funny had only so much overlap with what folks in the U.S. did.

In a way, that's the challenge in a nutshell that *any* company faces when it moves beyond its initial community, whether we're talking about a regional, national, or international expansion. In the U.S., when Starbucks arrives in a neighborhood, it is virtually indomitable. And yet the company famously fell on its rear end when it first jumped to Australia. The continent already had two major coffee chains that knew a lot better than a bunch of Seattle-ites what Aussies wanted in their cuppa.

One of the most dope businesses I've encountered recently is hyperlocal in nature. It's a payment app called Cinch Pay whose mission is to encourage communities to buy local. The irony of this hyperlocally oriented company is that its founder, Maya

Komerov, is Israeli, and until recently, she ran the whole thing from Tel Aviv. Doubling down on the irony, Maya chose Long Island, one of the most insular places on earth, as the beta testing ground for Cinch. But given its many small villages, each with its own Main Street and local identity, it's also easy to see the fit.

Here's how Cinch works: Shoppers load money to the app, which they can then spend at any locally owned business that's on the app. In return for paying with the app, they get anywhere between a 5 percent and 30 percent discount, depending on the shop. Cinch provides the shops with an interested audience of shoppers already in the app, free marketing, and data to help them figure out the right incentives. Businesses benefit from increased foot traffic, loyalty, and better cash flow to cover improvements and expansion.

"The big problem of the local economy is how to compete with the big boxes and chains," Maya says, adding that this is a world-wide disease, not an American affliction. "Cinch locks the money into the local economy. It's a tool to align interests and optimize the money flow in the community."

There was only the question of execution. As a heavily accented Israeli newcomer, pitching a payment app to shop owners while shaking the "go local" pom-poms was pretty much a no-go. Building an internal sales force wasn't an option either: too expensive, too hard to scale quickly. Maya understood right away that penetrating a foreign market requires more than understanding regional preferences. The deeper challenge, especially when your business involves financial transactions, is gaining trust.

"I could bring the tech, but I couldn't get the trust of the community in a reasonable time frame," says Maya. "So I thought, 'How can I provide the trust?' I needed to find the local influencers, the people whose asset is knowing the local community."

What she realized was that her cutting-edge fintech firm's perfect partner was very old-school: community newspapers. "They are old-fashioned businesses, but they have one very good thing. They are really trusted by the community, and they have strong relationships with the local businesses. So I made my first partnership with the Long Island *Herald*," says Maya. The *Herald*'s advertising sales team jumped into action, presenting Cinch's app to all their advertisers. In the summer of 2017, Rockville Centre, Long Island, became the first town to use Cinch. Soon after Lynbrook, Long Island, Williamsburg, Brooklyn, and downtown Manhattan were added. By early 2018 about 150 businesses and thousands of shoppers were using the platform, and at least fifty more towns will be using the app by the time this book goes to print.

As Maya made the transition to the U.S., her company changed internally, too. "I started with Israeli investors and an Israeli partner. When I saw where we were heading, I needed to think, 'Who are the right people to help make it happen?'" she says. She's the only Israeli on the executive team. Everyone else is American. "It was hard for them to make this shift and understand what we need to do with the local story." She has been traveling back and forth between Tel Aviv and the United States, but when last we spoke, she was getting ready to move her entire family—including her two kids, ages four and eight—to New York City. Her goal is to expand Cinch into 250 towns over a three-year period. "I think that we have the playbook to do that," she says.

If you're entering a new geography, you have to think like Maya: Who are your likeliest allies? Who wants you, needs you, and has the local influence to make their partnership matter? Cinch is giving small newspapers a chance to be relevant, allied with the latest and greatest tech in doing something really cool for their communities. And of course, it doesn't hurt that it's providing a new revenue stream in a difficult era for local advertising.

Thinking big picture, paradoxically, requires that you keep your eye on the little things. This means, as you expand, you've got to ensure your business is a win not just for customers but for every partner involved in the chain of bringing it to market.

Hack 49

Catch a Whale

The real revolution is always concerned with
the least glamorous stuff.   –Alice Walker

ONLY 2 PERCENT of America's women entrepreneurs make
more than a million dollars per year.[1] There's nothing wrong
with a small business, but if you want to grow big and grow fast,
Nina Vaca, the CEO of workforce solutions provider Pinnacle
Group, has the hack: Catch a whale. Make major corporations
and their procurement officers not just your clients but your
partners.

Nina, a five-foot-tall Ecuadorian powerhouse, started Pinnacle Group from her living room floor in 1996. Her story is a textbook how-to for anyone who wants to grow their business with
corporate clients. What started as a small, local company is now a
heavy-hitting multinational firm that wins and delivers major
contracts with iconic companies like AT&T, Verizon, and Comcast. Pinnacle has been on the *Inc.* 500/5000 list of fast-growing
private companies for more than a decade. In 2015, it was named
the fastest-growing women-owned/led company in the country
by the Women Presidents' Organization. As stunning as that
seems, it actually fits a pattern: According to the Women's Business Enterprise National Council (WBENC), women entrepreneurs who take on their first corporate client typically experience

an average increase in revenue of 266.4 percent over a period of two years. In Pinnacle's case, some years they grew as much as 350 percent!

People think it's hard to sell into a corporation. But try selling your product or service into a small company—or a dozen small companies—that has either a very small budget for what you're offering, or none at all. If you have, you already know what hard feels like. As Nina says, "Why go after fifty new customers when we can add one Fortune 500 that has a long-term and consistent need?"

You've got to offer something they need—preferably desperately. Nina's first job out of college was in IT in New York City, helping companies make the transition from mainframe computing to the UNIX operating system, a less expensive and more user-friendly solution. She saw that big companies like Goldman Sachs and Barclays were starving for IT workers. If top firms in a major metropolis were short of talent, she thought, imagine the challenge elsewhere. This was a rocket ship, and she hopped on. She gave notice, moved home to Texas, and started making calls, looking for companies that were migrating to UNIX.

She found immediate success with small, local clients. Five years after launch, she had grown the business to around $2 million in annual revenue—and had meanwhile been sowing seeds in a completely new ecosystem to help move to the next level. Nina joined organizations like the Women's Business Council Southwest (WBCS) and WBENC, whose sole purpose was to connect women with businesses like hers to major corporations that required more supplier diversity. I mentioned this strategy earlier in hack 9, Cash in on Your Woman Card.

Then came 9/11. The IT market went south. Companies were laying people off, not hiring them. Several of Pinnacle Group's competitors went out of business, but Nina survived. She had a liquidation plan in hand when the WBCS helped connect her with Verizon. And not just to anyone at Verizon, but to a supply chain procurement officer. These are the people who buy services in bulk for use across the business rather than in just one department. If scaling fast is your goal, there's no better way to get into large corporations than through their supply chains. That relationship changed everything.

"Let me tell you who some of the heroes of Pinnacle's story are," Nina says. "They are the chief procurement officer of Comcast, the chief procurement officer at Electronic Data Systems, the chief procurement officer at Unisys, to name a few. Those are the people who have given us tremendous opportunities to provide significant service in strategic areas that have helped us grow beyond my wildest dreams."

Of course, the introduction isn't everything—you've got to deliver, and, in Nina's words, be "crazy good" at what you do. "Once you have made a connection, you've got to do the homework to prove your value. If you don't know the business, then good luck with that," says Nina. "When I have a meeting with a prospective client, I already know the projects that are slated, their pain points, and their values. And I'm able to address every single one of those topics."

Pinnacle Group's ability to expand has been about more than landing corporate contracts. It's been about choosing customers carefully, looking for places where there's room to grow the relationship in the organization and over time. Once Nina has a new client, she implements a tried-and-true strategy: First, deliver exceptional service. Pinnacle is routinely named a top supplier by clients in multiple industries' supply chains. Second, provide a value that's larger than the product or service you're providing. "If all I provide is IT labor and workforce solutions, then I am just like everybody else. My hack has been to become so invaluable to the corporation that I'm not just a supplier, I'm a real partner."

Nina looks for clients who share her lifelong commitment to giving back and bettering the community. Take AT&T, for example, headquartered in Dallas, near Pinnacle. Over the years, they've partnered on community initiatives that go way beyond the IT space. Most recently, both served as industry partners with the Dallas Independent School District and the Dallas County Community College District's Pathways to Technology Early College High School (P-TECH) program, which allows traditionally underserved students to earn both a high school diploma and an associate's degree in four years, while gaining hands-on industry experience. "We have worked side by side with AT&T to improve lives, help students, and create the next generation of business leaders. This goes beyond business and gets to the heart of who we are," says Nina.

The challenge of catching a whale, of course, is making sure you're prepared to handle the giant beast. If you haven't prepared well for fast growth, it can be overwhelming. Two suggestions from Nina on how to prepare are:

1. **Start on Tier Two.** "Being a prime supplier to these Fortune 500 companies also means taking on a lot of risk overnight that can be challenging if you are not ready. If you don't have the right insurance, compliance, delivery model, and everything else, then you may be sorry that you're a prime. There are a lot of penalties, owner risks, and compliance issues. My secret was to start off as a Tier Two supplier—that's selling into one of the existing suppliers instead of directly to the corporation. That way, I'm protected from some of that risk. To me, it didn't matter whether the money was coming directly from the corporation or whether it was from a prime supplier. So I'd hunker down in Tier Two. I'm a triathlete, so I always have an analogy to athletics. In a race, you stay behind the person you want to beat. You stay close behind them, you watch their calves, and then about 200 yards before the finish line, you come out and you pass them. In the business context, you stay in Tier Two while you're learning the supply chain, meeting your financial goals, and learning how the company's procurement process works and how you can add value. You

gather a critical mass. Then, when you have it you can go to your procurement contact and say, 'I have critical mass, I add great value, here's why you need me as a prime supplier.'"

2. **Reinvest aggressively.** "Take your earnings and put them back into the business. I don't even know how many times I've said that. I've shouted it from the rooftops when I talk to women entrepreneurs, and nobody seems to understand it. Everybody wants to take money out of the company, run and buy the million-dollar house and the expensive cars, and they don't want to be disciplined. They don't want to delay gratification. They don't want to reinvest. Reinvestment into the company, especially at the early stage, is critical and massive if you want to scale.

"Fast growth can kill you if you don't reinvest in infrastructure. What's the technology that you're using to sustain your expansion? How many people do you have? What is the organizational model? What is your financial system? If you want to do business with a Fortune 500 company, they'll ask for your financials to verify that your house is in order and that your financial integrity is beyond reproach. If they see that you're not investing, they'll think you don't believe in yourself and that you don't believe in the company. And frankly, why should they?"

If this all sounds dizzying, remember that Nina started on the floor of her apartment with a service she knew big companies needed. If you have that kind of a business, the time to prepare is now. Find the seas to swim in where clients aren't a meal, they're food for an entire neighborhood. Make no mistake, my friend, this is not just how we play big, this is how we win. This is what we owe our communities and what the new revolution for women entrepreneurs is about. Because in the words of Alice Walker, "they must eat, revolution or not."

MICROHACK

Attention Global Founders

Are you an entrepreneur operating outside the United States? While organizations like WBENC are focused on connecting corporations with U.S.-based women-owned vendors, **Elizabeth Vazquez** has founded a similar organization to connect corporations with international suppliers. Check it out at **weconnectinternational.org**.

Hack 50

Do Good *and* Make Money

EARLIER I QUOTED advertising legend Cindy Gallop: "The future is doing good and making money simultaneously." Now, as you finish this book, hear it again. Imagine me increasing the bass of this particular beat.

Thinking that someday in the future as a wealthy mogul you'll sign Warren Buffett's Giving Pledge is no leapfrog. Neither is mistakenly thinking that nonprofits are the only way to change the world. Do good and make money simultaneously; *that's* the leapfrog. It's how you maximize impact, both in your pocket and in your community and maybe even beyond that.

Recently at a dinner I heard a sad cautionary tale about planned giving. With me at the table were a dozen or so of San Francisco's most generous philanthropists. My tablemate was a woman who spent ten years giving away all the money she'd made off the company she had spent the earlier part of her adult life building. You'd think she'd be sitting there proud and satisfied to have made a difference, right? No. She was deeply regretful. She had recently commissioned an impact study of all the organizations she had funded, and the results were horrifying to her: All that money she had given away couldn't be connected to any measurably improved social good. The net impact of all her work was zero.

So don't excuse complacency now by telling yourself about all the good you're going to do later. I'm not saying nonprofits or philanthropy can't improve lives, only that it's reductive to think of making money and doing good as mutually exclusive, or worse, at odds with each other.

Gale Epstein and Lida Orzeck, the founders of the world-famous high-end lingerie company Hanky Panky, are the fireworks and exclamation points and shiny balloon exemplars of Do Good and Make Money. That's why at Barnard's summer camp for high school entrepreneurs, one stop is always a tour of the central Hanky Panky warehouse and cutting floor in Jamaica, Queens.

Hanky Panky panties themselves are a rejection of another stupid either/or dichotomy, the idea that women have to choose between sexy and comfortable. These stretchy lace thongs are both. That's why the company, built from nothing, now sells a thong every ten seconds and around $50 million of underwear annually.

These savvy ladies never took a dollar of investment, and they never went public, so their financial details have always been private. What's clear as day to anyone who looks at the company, however, is the impact of the other two bottom lines that we should hold businesses to: social and ecological impacts.

Hanky Panky's factories are all in the northeastern United States. So unlike plenty of other companies, they don't leave a trail of CO_2 in the sky or battered sea life between here and some factory in Asia. They use packaging that's recyclable and 100 percent recycled paper in their offices. They make a quality product, not one that ends up in the bin after a couple of months of wear. Their employees are all covered by U.S. labor standards. And finally, their corporate philanthropy is renowned; almost one hundred different nonprofit organizations have received their support.

Hanky Panky employs 175 people. In 2017, those employees became the very first people to learn about Gale and Lida's exit plan, which the two had kept secret (from me, too!) for an entire year as they pulled the details together.

Lida and Gale are in their seventies, and many times I've ribbed Lida, "What's your exit plan, lady?" Ever since *The Wall Street Journal* ran a cover story in 2004 declaring the company's breakout success, they've had a steady stream of calls from financiers who want to either invest or buy them outright. Because what they love is running their company, they assigned someone else the task of taking the calls and saying, "Thank you, not interested." (Which is a lot nicer than what my pal Lida would have said to them: "My succession plan is eff you.")

Lida and Gale believed that if they sold, they wouldn't be able to protect the company and culture that they have created. "It's a pretty poorly kept secret that when you sell your company, no matter what promises people have made, it is going to change. It may become unrecognizable," says Lida.

Unrecognizable was unacceptable. And so for an entire year, Lida and Gale worked with their accounting team on a top secret plan for an alternative exit strategy. On October 12, as they celebrated their fortieth anniversary together with all their employees on the warehouse floor, they made an announcement. "We told them we were transferring ownership of the company to them," says Lida. "The employees paid nothing. But depending on when they were hired, almost everybody is becoming an immediate partial owner of the company."

Hanky Panky is now an employee stock ownership plan (ESOP), one of only about seven thousand in the United States. "It's like a 401(k) plan on steroids," says Gale. The two women remain in charge of the company, but they are now supervised by a board of trustees. The ESOP was the best means the pair could find to share their success with the people who built Hanky Panky.

When they shared the news at the party, not everyone immediately understood—not everybody there spoke English, let alone understood the complexities of an ESOP. But among the few people who got it, there was "a lot of weeping and wailing," Lida recalls.

Someday, you might consider an ESOP for your own alternative exit. But the real message here is that doing good is solid business practice that will serve you when you start and help you grow through every stage.

Oh, and another lesson from Gale and Lida, who were best friends for ten years before they started Hanky Panky. They didn't start the company with a clue of what it would or could become. "What was really driving us from the beginning was having a good time," says Gale. Hanky Panky started as a free, happy place where two founders, one a designer, could express themselves and their unique view of the world and how to treat the people in it. It's hard to imagine a bad crop coming from that fertile soil.

So get out there, plant your own seeds. Make money, do good, and for fuck's sake, HAVE FUN DOING IT!

Epilogue:
Go Forth, Be Brazen

It is no measure of health to be well adjusted to a
profoundly sick society. —Jiddu Krishnamurti

Y OU'VE FINISHED THE book. Now, leapfrog brazenly. Empha-
sis on *brazenly*. If I've convinced you that so-called shortcuts
aren't only justifiable but ingenious, then I can go to sleep happy.
The leapfrogs in the book are here whenever you need them, but
the real game going forward is in creating your own—which may
involve, at times, a gut check on core ethics and values. When
you're playing a game in which the rules are unjust, you have to
march a careful balance between fighting for better rules and doing what it takes to win.

Notice that I didn't include any of what you might call "white
hat" leapfrogs. White-hat hackers are the people who break into
security systems not to cause trouble but to reveal security flaws
and protect people. White-hat leapfrogs, then, are when you
take a step outside of your ethical norm as a kind of correction for
society's sickness. A few audacious examples I've heard recently
from friends:

- A woman marketing professional created three email aliases:
  Mary handled billing, Rebecca sent giveaway promotions,
  and Jason sent other marketing correspondence. This woman

had found she got better open rates on emails from names that were more traditional (read: WASPy) than her own "weird name," an idiosyncratic mash-up created by her Slavic parents. She also liked that it created the impression of the larger organization she was building toward.

- A solopreneur consultant got so sick of male competitors beating her out that she linked her maiden name with her married name and used it to rename her firm—two last names, giving the impression to major clients that she now had a male partner. It worked; she started landing bigger contracts, and by the time she was forced to come clean, she had the clout and track record to survive it.

- A woman author submitted her novel proposal to almost a dozen publishing firms and got rejected. She then submitted it with an initial as her first name, concealing her gender, and got offers from multiple houses.

You can't help but root for these audacious women. Yet it would be irresponsible for me to 100 percent endorse their tactics for a couple of reasons. Only *you* can decide which lines you're comfortable crossing. Also, these tactics are clearly provocative. They could backfire. Do you have the appetite for the potential negative attention? Again, that's for each of you to decide. Just make sure you're willing and able to someday defend your choice on the front page of *The New York Times*. This is a messy world full of idiots looking to put powerful women back "in their place." There are no secrets.

The truth is, you may not *need* white-hat hacks. I look at this same messy world and also see abundance and generosity. The more you look, the more you'll find leapfrogs that don't require crossing ethical lines. The more these leapfrogs will find *you*.

A State Department official recently reminded me where my own line falls. This man—we'll call him Gerry—sent me an email asking me to help recruit women entrepreneurs to attend a summit in India where they could meet potential investors and partners. It was an initiative started in the Obama White House, but that was then and this is now, and the host at this summit would be one Ivanka Trump. To participate would be to shake hands, however briefly, with the Trump administration.

When I balked, Gerry pushed back. The summit was a good enough leapfrog, he tried to convince me, that women entrepreneurs looking to scale globally should briefly make nice with the administration in order to attend. It was a fair point. But after thinking about it, I turned him down again. This was an aisle I wouldn't cross, not even for a minute. I want better for my fellow women than to have to align themselves, ever, with the basest elements of society in order to move forward. Further, this summit was far from the only opportunity in town—there were at least five other equally awesome upcoming events that I could direct women to. This particular event carried far too high a price for the group in our society that is, by every measure, the most entrepreneurial, the most promising, the most investment-worthy—and yet also among the most under attack by the Trump administration. *No, no, no, Gerry.* Still, I was appreciative to him for showing me my line and for provoking me to start a new campaign of donations to Planned Parenthood in Ivanka's name.

The question of legacy and how we will be remembered weighs heavily on me. How does one do business in a time of despots? As the inspiring Melissa Silverstein, founder of Women and Hollywood, often asks, what "cave paintings" will survive us and tell the world what we cared about and fought for? More urgent, what are we leaving for the next generation to inherit? As you move forward in your career, I hope this is a question you turn over as well, not once but often. As you know by now, it has led me to set very clear guidelines around what and to whom I'll commit myself. Our time is short, but the potential to contribute is great.

In the years since I committed to setting my own terms, what I've achieved while feeling ever more whole and authentic in the effort has *leapfrogged* wildly. I write this just days after giving my first-ever keynote in Spanish, a language that until now I used exclusively to navigate love and family—suddenly the door into a whole other sphere of influence has opened. And not only was the talk in Spanish, I gave it in Ecuador, my ancestral home. Planned Parenthood International had a summit in Quito and invited me to speak about investing in women's health. My dad watched proudly from the audience. Later, we traveled together to Cuenca and, after the little shake of a small earthquake, I settled in to find my own equator once again. Happiness, for me, is all of this.

The author Yrsa Daley-Ward once tweeted, "My destiny is louder than my comfort." We are living and loving in uncomfortable times—and there's no better time than now to join the fight. My wish for you, fellow revolutionary, is that you may stretch beyond comfort, find your own equator, and leapfrog into greatness.

Notes

INTRODUCTION

1 Bärí A. Williams, "The Tech Industry's Missed Opportunity: Funding Black Women Founders," LinkedIn, July 14, 2017, https://www .linkedin.com/pulse/diversity-opportunity-venture-capitalists-should -fund-williams.

2 American Express OPEN, *The 2016 State of Women-Owned Businesses Report*, April 2016, http://about.americanexpress.com/news/docs/2016x /2016SWOB.pdf.

3 Lisa Goodnight, "Research Indicates Pay Gap Will Not Close for 136 Years," September 13, 2016, The American Association of University Women. https://www.aauw.org/article/pay-gap-will-not-close-until -2152/.

HACK 1

1 Geri Stengel, "Why the Force Will Be with Women Entrepreneurs in 2016," *Forbes*, January 6, 2016, https://www.forbes.com/sites /geristengel/2016/01/06/why-the-force-will-be-with-women -entrepreneurs-in-2016.

2 Therese Huston, "Women Take More Risks than You Think—Which Makes Them a Better Investment," *Los Angeles Times*, July 12, 2016, http://www.latimes.com/opinion/op-ed/la-oe-huston-women-and-risk -20160711-snap-story.html.

HACK 3

1 Gail MarksJarvis, "Why Ariel's John Rogers Goes to McDonald's and What He Wants Kids to Know," *Chicago Tribune*, November 25, 2015, http://www.chicagotribune.com/business/ct-john-rogers-ariel -investments-1129-biz-20151125-story.html.

HACK 4

1 Laura J. Kray, Adam D. Galinsky, and Leigh Thompson, "Reversing the Gender Gap in Negotiations: An Exploration of Stereotype Regeneration," *Organizational Behavior and Human Decision Processes* 87, no. 2 (March 2002): 386–409, http://web.mit.edu/curhan/www/docs /Articles/15341_Readings/Social_Cognition/Kray_et_al_2002 _Reversing_the_gender_gap_in_negotiations.pdf.
2 Kelly Clay, "Why Millennial Women Are Burning Out," *Fast Company*, March 8, 2016, https://www.fastcompany.com/3057545/why -millennial-women-are-burning-out.

HACK 8

1 Elizabeth Currid-Halkett, "The New, Subtle Ways the Rich Signal Their Wealth," BBC, June 14, 2017, http://www.bbc.com/capital/story /20170614-the-new-subtle-ways-the-rich-signal-their-wealth.

HACK 10

1 Sheila Marikar, "At a Bay Area Club, Exclusivity Is Tested," *New York Times*, January 10, 2014, https://www.nytimes.com/2014/01/12/fashion /San-Francisco-club-Battery-Michael-Birch-Xochi-Birch.html.

HACK 12

1 Lee Seymour, "Broadway Gets Its Own Book Deal with Dress Circle Publishing," *Forbes*, August 4, 2015, http://www.forbes.com/sites /leeseymour/2015/08/04/broadway-gets-its-own-book-deal-with-dress -circle-publishing.

HACK 22

1   Tyrus Townsend, "Be Modern Man Ambassador: Meet 'The Change Agent' Trabian Shorters," *Black Enterprise*, June 13, 2016, http://www.blackenterprise.com/modern-man-meet-change-agent-trabian-shorters/.

HACK 26

1   Sloane Crosley, "Why Women Apologize and Should Stop," *New York Times*, June 23, 2015, https://www.nytimes.com/2015/06/23/opinion/when-an-apology-is-anything-but.html.

HACK 27

1   Dana Kanze et al., "Male and Female Entrepreneurs Get Asked Different Questions by VCs—and It Affects How Much Funding They Get," *Harvard Business Review*, June 27, 2017, https://hbr.org/2017/06/male-and-female-entrepreneurs-get-asked-different-questions-by-vcs-and-it-affects-how-much-funding-they-get.

HACK 33

1   Kanyi Maqubela, "The Rise of Startups . . . or Not," LinkedIn, November 29, 2017, https://www.linkedin.com/pulse/rise-startups-kanyi-maqubela.

HACK 35

1   Ruth Simon, "Kickstarter Closes the 'Funding Gap' for Women," *Wall Street Journal*, August 13, 2014, https://www.wsj.com/articles/kickstarter-closes-the-funding-gap-for-women-1407949759.
2   J. D. Alois, "On CircleUp, Women Founders are 5X More Successful Compared to Raising Money from VCs," *Crowdfund Insider*, June 4, 2015, https://www.crowdfundinsider.com/2015/06/68922-on-circleup-women-founders-are-5x-more-successful-compared-to-raising-money-from-vcs/.

HACK 40

1   U.S. Small Business Administration Office of Advocacy, "Frequently Asked Questions About Small Business," August 2017, https://www

.sba.gov/sites/default/files/advocacy/SB-FAQ-2017-WEB.pdf?utm
_medium=email&utm_source=govdelivery.

HACK 43

1   Katharine Zaleski, "I'm Sorry to All the Mothers I Worked With,"
    Fortune.com, March 3, 2015, http://fortune.com/2015/03/03/female
    -company-president-im-sorry-to-all-the-mothers-i-used-to-work-with.

HACK 46

1   U.S. Census Bureau, "New Census Bureau Report Analyzes U.S.
    Population Projections," March 3, 2015, https://www.census.gov
    /newsroom/press-releases/2015/cb15-tps16.html.

HACK 49

1   Eilene Zimmerman, "Only 2% of Women-Owned Businesses Break the
    $1 Million Mark—Here's How to Be One of Them," *Forbes*, April 1,
    2015, https://www.forbes.com/sites/eilenezimmerman/2015/04/01
    /only-2-of-women-owned-businesses-break-the-1-million-mark-heres
    -how-to-be-one-of-them.

Resources

Books, organizations, and other resources for entrepreneurs, from the pages of *Leapfrog*.

BOOKS

The Creative Habit: Learn It and Use It for Life by Twyla Tharp. New York: Simon & Schuster, 2006.

Drop the Ball: Achieving More by Doing Less by Tiffany Dufu. New York: Flatiron Books, 2017.

The E-Myth Revisited: Why Most Businesses Don't Work and What to Do About It by Michael Gerber. New York: Harper Collins, 2004.

Getting to Yes: How to Negotiate Agreement Without Giving In (2nd ed.) by Roger Fisher, William Ury, and Bruce Patton. New York: Penguin Books, 1991.

No Excuses: Nine Ways Women Can Change How We Think About Power by Gloria Feldt. New York: Seal Press, 2012.

Playing Big: Practical Wisdom for Women Who Want to Speak Up, Create, and Lead by Tara Mohr. New York: Avery, 2015.

Predictably Irrational: The Hidden Forces That Shape Our Decisions (rev. ed.) by Dan Ariely. New York: Harper Perennial, 2010.

Reach: 40 Black Men Speak on Living, Leading, and Succeeding by Ben Jealous and Trabian Shorters (ed.). New York: Atria, 2015.

Self-Made: Becoming Empowered, Self-Reliant, and Rich in Every Way by Nely Galán. New York: Spiegel & Grau, 2016.

What Works: Gender Equality by Design by Iris Bohnet. Cambridge: Belknap Press, 2016.

CERTIFICATION

National Minority Supplier Development Council: Advances business opportunities for certified minority business enterprises and connects them to corporate members. Website: http://www.nmsdc.org.

Small Business Administration: Helps Americans start, build, and grow businesses. Website: https://www.sba.gov.

Women's Business Enterprise National Council (WBENC): Offers world-class standard of certification to women-owned businesses throughout the country. Website: http://www.wbenc.org.

COMMUNITY BUILDING AND SOCIAL IMPACT

Breakout: Breakout's aim is to unite, inspire, and amplify those using their lives to make the world a better place. Website: http://www.breakout.today.

Daybreaker: An early morning dance movement in eighteen cities around the world and growing. Website: https://www.daybreaker.com.

Nexus: Global movement to bridge communities of wealth and social entrepreneurship. Website: https://nexusglobal.org.

Planned Parenthood: Family planning and women's health services, along with resources and advocacy for women's rights. Website: https://www.planned parenthood.org.

Sundance Film Festival: Celebrating independence, creativity, and risk-taking, the Sundance Film Festival plays a vital role in identifying emerging international talent and connecting them with audiences and industry in the United States. Website: https://www.sundance.org/festivals/sundance -film-festival.

TED: Nonprofit devoted to spreading ideas, usually in the form of short, powerful talks (eighteen minutes or less). Website: https://www.ted.com.

United State of Women: The United State of Women is dedicated to being the megaphone for the gender equality movement. Website: https://www .theunitedstateofwomen.org.

CONFERENCE

TEDxWomen: Meaningful conversation about the power of girls and women. Website: https://www.ted.com/participate/organize-a-local-tedx-event/before-you-start/event-types/tedxwomen.

CROWDFUNDING

CircleUp: Equity crowdfunding site based in San Francisco. Website: https://circleup.com.

Crowdfunder: Equity crowdfunding site that allows you to set your own terms. Website: https://www.crowdfunder.com.

Kickstarter: Funding for a wide array of projects. Website: https://www.kickstarter.com.

New York Angels: One of the longest-running active angel groups in New York City; it has invested more than $100 million in entrepreneurial ventures. Website: http://www.newyorkangels.com.

Seed&Spark: A crowdfunding site for film entrepreneurs. Website: https://www.seedandspark.com.

EDUCATION

The Athena Center for Leadership Studies: Educational program associated with Barnard College. Website: https://athenacenter.barnard.edu.

Entrepreneurs-in-Training: Barnard's pre-college summer program for young female entrepreneurs through the Athena Summer Innovation Institute. Website: https://barnard.edu/summer/ASII.

General Assembly: Innovative training for lifelong learning and success in technology fields such as coding, product development, and marketing. Website: https://generalassemb.ly/.

Gotham Gal: Investor Joanne Wilson's blog, including links to her podcast. Website: https://gothamgal.com/.

Maker's Row: Simplifies the manufacturing process by helping you learn about manufacturers, by connecting you to the right ones, and by managing the production process. Website: https://makersrow.com.

Pipeline Angels: Pipeline Angels is changing the face of angel investing and creating capital for women and non-binary femme social entrepreneurs—anyone identifying with womanhood (cis, trans, third gender). Website: http://pipelineangels.com.

Skillcrush: Provides resources to increase one's knowledge of technology. Website: https://skillcrush.com.

MUTUAL BENEFIT SOCIETIES AND PEER NETWORKS

Black Female Founders (#BFF): Black Female Founders (#BFF) is a global membership organization, community, and movement for women-led tech ventures and female tech leaders throughout the Black Diaspora. Website: http://www.blackfemalefounders.org.

BMe: An award-winning network of community-builders known for defining people by their positive contributions to society and enlisting incredible black men who inspire us to be better together. Website: http://www.bme community.org.

The Collective (of Us): An online accelerator and community for women business owners. Website: https://www.thecollectiveofus.com.

Dreamers // Doers: High-impact membership community for trailblazing women. Website: http://www.dreamersdoers.me.

SheWorx: A global platform and event series empowering 20,000+ female entrepreneurs to build and scale successful companies. Website: https://www.sheworx.com.

Women Who Tech: A nonprofit organization bringing together talented and renowned women breaking new ground in technology to transform the world and inspire change. Website: https://www.womenwhotech.com.

TALENT RESOURCES

Catalyte: Uses artificial intelligence to identify individuals, regardless of background, who have the innate potential and cognitive ability to be great software developers. Website: https://catalyte.io.

Jopwell: A leading career advancement platform for black, Latinx/Hispanic, and Native American students and professionals. Website: https://www.jopwell.com.

PowerToFly: Connects Fortune 500 companies and fast-growing startups with women who are looking to work for companies that value gender diversity and inclusion. Website: https://powertofly.com.

The Muse: Online career resources, from dream jobs to career advice. Website: https://www.themuse.com.

VC FIRMS, INCUBATORS, AND ACCELERATORS

Avante Mezzanine Partners: Avante Mezzanine Partners provides total debt solutions and junior capital for high-quality, lower middle market businesses that generate at least $3 million in cash flow. Website: http://www.avantemezzanine.com.

Backstage Capital: Invests in companies led by underrepresented founders. Website: http://backstagecapital.com.

Kapor Capital: Oakland-based social impact investment firm. Website: http://www.kaporcapital.com.

Pipeline Angels: Changing the face of angel investing and creating capital for women and non-binary femme social entrepreneurs. Website: http://pipelineangels.com.

SheEO: A leader in global innovation in the female entrepreneur marketplace. Website: https://sheeo.world.

Trendseeder: Accelerator that invites a select number of fashion, beauty, and health and wellness entrepreneurs to participate in an intensive curriculum program. Website: https://www.trendseeder.com.

Acknowledgments

The seed for this book was planted by three intergenerational groups of women (we called them Masterminds) that I curated as part of an experiment at the Athena Center for Leadership Studies at Barnard College. It started in response to a request from a student, an extraordinary civic entrepreneur, Lulu Mickelson, who craved a peer group. The first mastermind, a once-a-month dinner group geared towards entrepreneurs (four students, four adults), was so successful that we built another one the following year, and then a third focused on women in the corporate world. Among our long list of milestones, we supported one of the students, the amazing Eva Sasson, through the sale of her first tech startup her junior year. We also watched Adda Birnir as she grew her tech upskilling startup, Skillcrush. We nurtured Emily-Anne Rigal's literary aspirations and helped her sell her first book, based on her first startup, WeStopHate, started in high school. We encouraged Avani Patel as she pivoted her company, Trendseeder, and we assisted Elise Schuster as her sex-positive app business took shape. We banded together to help Jada Hawkins with whatever ten startups she was working on in any given week, and we jumped for joy when Miranda Stamps quit her corporate job and announced a plan to travel the outback of Australia with her husband and two kids. An exceptional community was created, and as the success stories piled up it became clear to me and my cofounder at Entrepreneurs@Athena, our resident feminist icon, the amazing Kitty Kolbert, that we needed this model, and the magic it created, to scale.

But how do you scale the careful curation of magical mastermind groups that seem to consistently propel women forward into success? Operationally, it would be too hard to replicate widely, so Kitty suggested we give women the tools to do it themselves and just write the how-to book. Being a storyteller, I thought the best way to show people how to do it is to illustrate how others have. To tell their stories.

Multiple iterations of the book proposal later, the list of women whose stories I wanted to tell had grown. Eventually, the book extended beyond Athena and even started to include some wonderful men. In the end, it wasn't even a book about mastermind groups, meeting for dinner once a month for two semesters. It became a book that took all the world-changing wisdom from my extraordinary collection of brilliant humans, and distilled it into fifty tools built from the ground up, to serve women entrepreneurs or any misfits who want to do business their own way. But make no mistake, the inspiration for this book started with this inimitable community and the secret sauce from that college on a hilltop in Morningside. So, first and foremost, thank you to the OG Athena Masterminders (Cathy O'Neil, Avani Patel, Deborah Berebichez, Jovanka Ciares, Lulu Mickelson, Eva Sasson, Olivia Benjamin, Sarosh Arif, Toby Milstein, Jada Hawkins, Emily-Anne Rigal, Elise Schuster, Adda Birnir, Roberta Pereira, Kavita Mehra, Virginie Henry-Dise, Kris Cottom, Clara Rodriguez, Miranda Stamps, Kate Voyeton, Jenn Shaw, and the woman who once said she'd bury a body for me, Shala Burroughs). I am so grateful to the Athena Center team and the greater Barnard community. Thank you Kitty, for welcoming me and for being my Dolores Huerta.

To every Barnard student and my Athena Digital Design Agency rock stars, you have brightened my days and fueled my determination to clear the path for the magnificence you bring to the world. I am forever changed because of you. You are my *why*, each and every one of you, including Jada Hawkins, Wynnie Newton, Shelby Lane, Monica Powell, Amiah Sheppard, Lauren Beltrone, Naomi Tewodros, Carmen Ren, Amal Abid, Anastasia Rab, Elizabeth de Luna, Olivia Benjamin, Kate Brea, Stephanie Rothermal, Shaday Fermin, Cassidy Mayeda, Danielle Deluty, Lyndsie Anderson (BRAVA web mistress), Sara Kim, and Mica Spicka (thank you for being Lila's second mom).

While inspiration is the fuel for life, fuel only works when you've got a machine that knows how to use it and make shit happen. That machine is my *Leapfrog* founding team: hands down the most dedicated agent in the world, Joy Tutela from the David Black Literary Agency, and the most patient and sublime cocreator I could ever have asked for, Sara Grace. Books, in my experience, are a slog. I came to believe that authors, like mothers, are genetically built to forget the birth process, otherwise they'd never write another book. No matter the talent or the great intentions of a team, every publishing effort I've been directly or indirectly involved in has had its unpleasant kinks and its unexpected and often dramatic twists and turns. Every effort, that is, until this one. A big reason for that is the spectacular TarcherPerigee team, starting with Stephanie Bowen, and then my wonderful editor, Nina Shield, along with Marlena Brown, Roshe Anderson, and Hannah Steigmeyer. I'm humbled to have your enthusiastic support and wisdom at the table. But before we ever talked to a publisher, the foundation for goodness was already there. From the kindness and deep respect that Joy brings to every interaction, to her absurdly heroic emails when the book went to auction just as she was going into the hospital to deliver her third child, my agent Joy shows up every damn day and delivers the equivalent energy of a small army. Then (and I say this knowing full well that it will not be believed, but with the conviction of someone who has seen the mountaintop and will not deny its existence), to have cowritten an entire book, and to have invited an eccentric cast of dozens of wildly different humans into the creative process, and to be able to truthfully say that there was not a moment in the process that was not an absolute, unequivocal delight, is a small miracle that only Sara Grace could have made real. I can't explain it, because I always believed that creation needed to be a struggle and that even when the muse shows up, the path is never straight and without effort. And yet, with Sara by my side, I can honestly say that it has been the pleasure of a lifetime, from beginning to end, without exception. And thanks to her, there will definitely be other books.

As the project grew, so did the team. It started with BRAVA's very first brilliant intern, Aditi Somani, followed by the heavy lift of the Atlanta powerhouse, Maleni Somani, who for a glorious year was my right hand, and followed gracefully by the one person who has probably read more pre-published versions of this book than anyone else, the wonderful Molly Cavanaugh. *Leapfrog* has been nurtured by brilliant young minds throughout, and is better for it.

In the time since the original idea for *Leapfrog* surfaced BRAVA was also born, and with it came a new community of dedicated supporters who have not only contributed insight but also helped shape and adjust ideas that were sometimes hotly debated and often morphed as a result. They include my personal finance tutor, Robert Farrokhnia, to my loyal friend and business strategist,

Patrick Mitchell, to Denielle Sachs, who helped frame our business universe, to Bianca Caban, who authored the first pitch, and my friend-wife Jovanka Ciares, who heroically stepped in to help me keep the ship afloat. Trevor Neilson, Todd Morley, Howard Buffett, and the whole team at i(x) investments were the first to believe in and get behind BRAVA, more evidence that we had nothing but excellence at the table from day 1. And because, when things get busy, we prefer to build a bigger table than a taller fence, we've had the honor of welcoming some of the best in the world, including coconspirators who joined in on the ground floor including Mirella Levinas, Mariana Huberman, Lida Orzeck, Kat Cole, Brendan Doherty, Deborah Borg, Xochi Birch, Ori Sasson, and Rich Colton. And also, the most insanely wise and talented group of business advisors an overly inquisitive CEO could ever ask for, including Kathryn Kolbert (sense a theme?), James Benedict, Jimmie Briggs, Wendy Davidson, Erin Erenberg, James Peréz Foster, Nely Galán, Spencer Gerrol, Galia Gichon, Kat Gordon, Susie Greenwood, Sue Heilbronner, David Homan, Eason Jordan, Kerry Kennedy, Lynn Loacker, Tolu Olubunmi, Jo Ousterhout, Nathalie Rayes, Alyson Richards, Nina Vaca, Robyn Ward, and the legendary Marie C. Wilson. The list of informal advisors is an embarrassment of riches but I must give special thanks to the ones who have kindly taken more calls from me than is probably appropriate: Tina Tchen, Ambassador Attallah Shabazz, Ann Lawrence, Rachel Gerrol Cohen, Michael McKenna Miller, Joan Fallon, Doug Spencer, Alejandra Duque Cifuentes, Molly Dewolf Swenson, Gloria Feldt, Lela Goren, and Marla Smith. Thank you for being my rocks. Thank you Valerie Varco for being there consistently, and welcome Nolwenn Delisle—I hope we continue the collaboration as long as your father and I did—we had a good run! To the newest additions to the BRAVA family, Nap Hosang, Samantha Miller, Malcolm Potts, Dar Rosario, Katherine Pence, and Eileen Carey, welcome and thank you for your trust. Gratitude also goes to the extended BRAVA family, including Gratitude Railroad, the Glenmede team, and the badasses at The United State of Women; thank you for letting us be born on your stage in 2016.

I'm humbled by and grateful to you, Tanya Malott, for always seeing me in the most beautiful light; you don't make portraits, you illuminate. The references I've included to the book *Self Made* are especially meaningful thanks to the extraordinary force of nature who is Nely Galán. I remain delighted and proud to have had the opportunity to support you in creating your most generous legacy. Knowing I always have your fierceness in my corner helps me sleep at night.

Aging being a privilege denied to many, I'm honored to enter a stage in life in which mentees are beginning to surface, sometimes from the most unexpected places and usually involuntarily, when they inform me that I am now advising them (damn, I love me a bossy woman). Among those who have honored me with the distinction are Emily Kelleher-Best, Victoria Flores, Lauren Bonner, Jackie Rotman, Vanessa Alexandra Pestritto, Namibia Donadio, Robyn Moreno, Erin Bernhardt, Isa Watson, Arianna Afsar, Denise Hewett, and yes, the occasional extraordinary dude, like Gabriel Rodriguez, Michael Farber, and the man who will soon take over the world with his own kind and generous revolution, Chris Wilson.

My favorite life hack of all, and the reason I plan to outlive most of you (sorry not sorry), is one familiar to many women (also probably why we all live longer), my girl friends. They're my greatest passion and my highest priority, as is proper. I'll start with my first friend, Mayra Molina, no relation but she may as well have been. Then there are my friend-wives, "the coven" who keep me grounded and sometimes a little dusty with playa love (Kat, Sheida, Jovanka, and Neeta). And, of course, my Colombian soul sister Carla Perez Henao, who neither distance nor silence can ever remove from my heart. Big love goes to the posse I'm lucky to have on speed dial and group texts, usually ready for mischief, a crisis, or just heart emojis, including Vanessa Fajans-Turner, Hitha Palepu, Michelle Arevalo-Carpenter, Nancy and Karen Bong, Joya Dass, Rakia Reynolds, Carrie Hammer, Tracey Fischer, Jess Weiner, Chef Grace Ramirez, Melissa Silverstein, Rha Goddess, Mally Steves Chakola, Diana Franco, Elise Hernandez (Santora), Morgan Simon, Joy Gorman Wettels, Kimberly Bryant, Danielle Feinberg (now dubbed Oscar mama), Erin Vilardi, Ella Quinlan, Julie Ann Crommett, Heather Mason, Natalia Oberti Noguera, Nercy Sullivan, Gayle Jennings-O'Byrne, Whitney Smith, Michelle Herrera Mulligan, Candice Cook Simmons, Sophia Danenberg, Tizita Asefa, Danielle Posa, Suzanne Biegel, the honorable Nora Vargas, and our very own goddess, Christa Bell.

Because I'm South American and *big* isn't the right word for how large our clans are, I will simply thank them all, from Bogotá, Cuenca, Madrid, Los Angeles, and every other corner, for tolerating, nurturing, humoring, and in all other ways making the life I live, and the love with which I live it, possible. Special *abrazos* to my *queridas*, Awilda Verdejo, Anyela Hernandez, Patricia Peñafiel, *abuelita* Anita, Maria Isabel Gil, Maria Soledad Solano, Michelle Molina, Kathy Frisan, my sister Nicolle, and my girl, the apple of my eye, forever my wunderkid, Sophia Barriga Hernandez.

Times like these make even the most optimistic among us wonder what on earth is wrong with men these days. Thankfully, in my case, I don't have to look far to see evidence of everything that manhood should and will someday be, if we all do what generations after us need us to do. If I was into praying, and if I ever fell on my head and decided to pray to a male deity, the following would be the men around whom I hope we'd be smart enough to build a new cosmology. Thank you Daveed Diggs, Wayne Escoffery, Michael Blake, Vishal Sapra, Andy Fife, Daniel P. Johnston, Milton Speid, Greg Shell, Nathan Proctor, Isaiah Johnson, Ashoka Finley, Ritchard Wooley, Kenny Pulsifer, Mike Masserman, Trabian Shorters, Denmark West, Brendan Doherty, Cannon Hersey, Adam Cummings, Caleb Gardner, Daley Ervin, Scott Beale, Perfecto Sanchez, Rob Salkowitz, Justin Goldbach, Brent Sweet, Jon Day, Sami Chester, Citi Medina, Sean Hairston, Cesar Barriga, and my two oldest buddies, who have been on this ride since I was a teenager, Mads Galsgaard and Olivier Oosterbaan, for simply being you, and especially for honoring me with your friendship.

To the leapfroggers, I hope I did your stories justice, and that every person who sees them can sense the respect and care with which we tried to serve them up to the world, where they belong and are much needed.

Jennie Falco, thank you for keeping me sane and grounded and, failing that, keeping me grounded in my moments of insanity.

My dearest Tolu, you're everything that the United States should aspire to one day become. Thank you for gracing it, and me, with your presence, and may every one of your big dreams soon be realized.

Finally, Mami and Papi, in the words of Stanislaw Jerzy Łec, "No snowflake in an avalanche ever feels responsible." You are my quiet, soft snowflakes in a storm, and you are my agitators in moments of complacency. You are forward movement embodied. Most of all, you, your struggles, your courage, your humility, and your love are what I am most proud of in the whole world. The best decision I've ever made was choosing you, the best leapfrog of all.

About the Authors

Nathalie Molina Niño is the CEO and founder of BRAVA Investments, investing in high-growth, innovative businesses that deliver a measurable economic benefit to women. A technologist and coder by training, Molina Niño launched her first tech startup at the age of twenty. Molina Niño is also the cofounder of Entrepreneurs@Athena at the Athena Center for Leadership Studies of Barnard College at Columbia University. She has served as a business and global growth advisor to industry leaders in the for-profit and nonprofit sectors, including Disney, Microsoft, MTV, Mattel, and the Bill & Melinda Gates Foundation. Most recently, she stepped in as CRO of PowerToFly and led the launch campaign for Nely Galán's *New York Times* bestseller and company, Self-Made.

Sara Grace is a New York–based author and editorial partner to entrepreneurs, artists, and earth-shakers. Find her at saragrace editorial.com.